Amy
Carmichael

WOMEN OF FAITH SERIES

Amy Carmichael
Corrie ten Boom
Florence Nightingale
Gladys Aylward
Isobel Kuhn
Mary Slessor

MEN OF FAITH SERIES

Borden of Yale
Brother Andrew
C. S. Lewis
Charles Finney
Charles Spurgeon
Eric Liddell
George Muller
Hudson Taylor
Jim Elliot
Jonathan Goforth
John Hyde
John Wesley
Samuel Morris
Terry Waite
William Carey

John and Betty Stam

Amy Carmichael

Kathleen White

BETHANY HOUSE PUBLISHERS
MINNEAPOLIS, MINNESOTA 55438
A Ministry of Bethany Fellowship, Inc.

Amy Carmichael
Kathleen White

Library of Congress Catalog Card Number 92–81655

ISBN 1–55661–302–4

Copyright © 1986
Kathleen White
All Rights Reserved

Originally published in English by Marshall Morgan &
Scott Publications Ltd. now part of HarperCollins Publishers Ltd. under the title *Amy Carmichael*

Published by Bethany House Publishers
A Ministry of Bethany Fellowship, Inc.
6820 Auto Club Road, Minneapolis, Minnesota 55438

Printed in the United States of America

Contents

1

Childhood Years

I wish ... oh how I wish!" Most children are familiar with the old fairy tale of three wishes that a foolish old man and his wife wasted due to their greed and stupidity. One little girl would have been well content with only a single wish granted. At three years of age, she was already old enough to have decided color preferences, and her greatest disappointment was that she had been born with brown eyes when she really longed for blue, to be like her mother.

From as far back as she could remember, her mother had impressed one thing on her: "Ask God, Amy, if you want anything badly. Share it with Him. He's never too far away to hear our prayers and He'll always give you an answer."

This seemed the ideal solution to Amy, so she knelt down and in simple childish faith begged God to change the color of her eyes.

So implicit was her trust in her Heavenly Father, she never doubted that the transformation would be effected by the morning. Upon waking, she climbed confidently out of bed and scrambled up to kneel on the seat of a chair she had pushed against the chest of drawers. Her eager, happy smile was reflected back at her from the mirror, but the eyes above the curving mouth remained a deep, dark brown.

Instead of feeling devastated because her hopes were not realized, her initial disappointment was replaced with the impression that God hadn't let her down after all. Neither had He failed to answer, just as her mother had promised. At that moment Amy dimly knew that "No" could also be an answer. God had surely heard, but sometimes He says "Wait" or "No" rather than an immediate "Yes."

What she couldn't appreciate at the time was what an asset those despised brown eyes would prove to be in the far-off future. God had a very good reason for saying "No" on that occasion. She had learned too a valuable lesson about Him, and she would be able to draw on that knowledge at other times of crisis and disappointments later on. Amy never underestimated the importance of that experience, and when she was older she wrote a poem about it, which was included in one of her books.

She need never have mentioned it again because it was only a fleeting, childish incident, but probably she decided to put it on record for posterity to help other children in their relationship with God. Perhaps they would understand better how He answered prayer when they had read a simple, real-life story. And children were what mattered most of all to Amy, right from the start. Years afterward, as she set off in search of poor, ill-used Temple children in India, Amy would stain her hands and arms and any other exposed area of skin with coffee, and put on an Indian sari so she could enter places where foreign women would be prohibited. Usually, she escaped detection, but had she possessed blue eyes she would have been recognized immediately as English. So God had a special purpose in creating little Amy just as she was, and she never tired of telling the Indian children in her care this story.

Amy was born on December 16, 1867, to David and Catherine Carmichael, who welcomed the arrival of their first of seven children with great joy and thanksgiving. David had not married until he was thirty-seven years old. He and his brother William had worked by day helping to run two mills, the Upper and the Lower, close to the sea at Millisle, County Down, in Northern Ireland. In their precious spare time, they supported the activities of the local Presbyterian minister, John Beatty, even giving him over £500—a large sum of money in those days—to build a schoolhouse. This was used for day and evening classes and services on Sunday evenings.

William and his wife had five children, so there was soon no shortage of companions for Amy, who was often ringleader in their many escapades. Far from behaving like a typical, prim little Victorian miss, she frequently tore around in a tomboyish fashion. On one occasion, she crawled out onto the tiles with two of her brothers, intent on walking around a lead gutter that skirted the roof. No doubt she found it difficult to explain the impulse to her parents after climbing down through the skylight again!

In spite of being dressed in the many layers of constricting clothes that Victorian children wore, Amy didn't hesitate to lead other playmates to stand on the seawall and get deliciously drenched with the wild sea spray. Although she had to face up to punishment for her pranks afterward, Amy never sulked or resented it. She knew it was only what she deserved.

On the other hand, Amy's father brought her up to be tough, teaching her to swim tied by a rope to a safety belt, and to ride a lively pony, which took a great deal of managing. "I am grateful to my father for teaching me never to give in to a difficulty," she wrote as an adult, having experienced the same sort of treatment as Charles Studd, the famous missionary, had given his four daughters in India. Strangely enough, Amy would meet those four girls years later in India, at their outdoor baptism.

Amy learned physical endurance, stick-to-itiveness, and obedience—all qualities she would need when she grew up and embarked upon her career of service. Her parents were anxious, too, that Amy and her brothers and sisters should become aware of the needs of others. From early childhood they were sent down to the village with nourishing soup for the sick and destitute. Sometimes the children resented their errand when it meant leaving their own meal until after their return home—it was impossible to hurry and arrive with a full canister of the hot liquid. But however much they grumbled, it always seemed worthwhile when the grateful old villagers thanked them for their efforts. State social care was practically nonexistent in those days. Acts of charity were usually left to the wives of parsons, rich landowners, doctors and industrialists. So like Florence Nightingale and Edith Cavell, they learned to care first by small acts of kindness locally to the aged and infirm.

Yet Amy's parents were not just content to teach her to live by a moral code; they both possessed a deep personal faith in the Lord Jesus Christ. Naturally they were anxious to pass this on—not impose it on their children—and from her earliest years Amy was made aware of God's love and His claims on her life. Although church-going was fashionable in Victorian times and many people attended mainly because it was socially acceptable, Amy's parents found real joy and happiness in going to services. Instead of regarding church attendance as a conventional, formal duty, for them it became the highlight of the week. The fact that the local minister was also a family friend who stepped in to play chess with their father, helped the children get to know him personally and not just look up to him as a distant figure in the pulpit on Sundays.

"And yet we got endless fun out of life," recorded Amy. She learned to take the rough with the smooth, to accept the punishment if she had behaved badly according to grown-up standards; ". . . the game was worth the candle." Yet she felt hurt if she had upset her mother too badly, and hastened to make matters right with her again. Often later in life she would tell her little children in India tales of her own childhood. It is likely that she devoted her life to caring for children and trying to improve their lot because of her own happy early years. It made her sad to see tiny ones deprived of all she had enjoyed: the loving home and caring parents. Little did she know as a girl that in her adult life she would become substitute mother to many hundreds of children.

So Amy developed, not as a model child, but normal and natural with several contrasts in her character. The many governesses that the Carmichaels employed before the children were sent to school met with varying success and a mixed reception from their pupils. Amy took an instant dislike to one and joined her brothers and sisters in making her job so difficult that she was forced to resign, much to their relief. This same Amy, however, displayed great sympathy and gentleness toward anyone who was ill.

All the children loved to hear stories and listened avidly to anyone who spent time with them spinning yarns. One lady taught them to recite poems by heart, which may have stimulated Amy's interest in writing verse and kindled her love for rhyming words and lilting meters. She also told the children stories about martyrs from among their Scottish Covenanter forebears.

Another welcome visitor at the Carmichael home was the brother of the Rev. John Beatty, their local minister. As a missionary in India, he came home on furlough for a year and stayed at a house close to his brother's manse. On Sunday afternoons he and his wife used to tell the children stories about India and Amy seemed particularly interested, often staying on after the others to beg for more.

Without the benefit of modern media, both the Carmichael families led full and happy lives. Entertainment had to be homemade but it was none the worse for that. They enjoyed their nearness to both the rolling ocean and the lovely Irish countryside stretching beyond their village. Their parents were sufficiently affluent to allow them a comfortable home and ponies to ride, yet the children never became spoiled because of their circumstances. From infancy, they were taught to share their possessions, and no class distinction was ever observed in the Carmichael home.

Anyone who needed encouragement, regardless of status, would be asked to the house for a meal. Amy's mother volunteered to teach some of the older girls cooking and singing. David took an interest in the boys, often personally recommending them to owners of businesses in Belfast. Millisle had little to offer in the way of jobs apart from limited employment in the mills, but he felt a concern for the local boys and often took on the responsibility of trying to fix them up with work.

Both David and William were men of enterprise and vision and not afraid to introduce new technology. Steam power was added, the roller system for grinding wheat was brought in, and gas lighting was installed. The wheat itself was imported from America and came to Ireland via Liverpool. Business prospered and it seemed as though their new experiments were bringing success and prosperity to the two owners.

To Amy and her brothers and sisters the future looked assured—if they ever stopped to think about it. All the cousins enjoyed happy companionship with each other. Their parents were respected members of the community and yet regarded with great affection. From their infancy the children had known the comfort and security of the love of God explained to them and lived out practically by the grown-ups. They were surrounded by the natural beauty of the lovely Irish landscape, and with lively, fertile imaginations they never felt at a loss for activities, even if some of them led the children into scrapes.

But change was in store for them, and life would never be quite so carefree and happy again. Still, those early years provided Amy with a rich store of happy memories, and many were the anecdotes that she in turn passed on to her little ones years later in far away India. Being scrupulously honest, she told them also about the times when she grieved her parents, but the overall picture is one of a happy, caring relationship within the family, the church, and the whole village community.

Yet, the well-worn expression is true that all good things come to an end, and this was one of the earliest lessons Amy had to face. At the time, she couldn't have known just what this would involve for all of them. In spite of the intervening years and miles, she was never to forget these early recollections of things held especially dear to her. They still remained clear and vivid enough in her imagination to be recorded in her book *Kohila*. ". . . a child had listened to the talk of the sailors who looked after the little yachts . . . moored near the shore of Strangford Lough. The good smell of salt water, the good sight of honest faces and rough blue jerseys, the sound of lapping water are to this day mixed in her mind with those talks which often dealt with greater things than boats."

2

An Irish Youth

To further his business interests, David Carmichael moved with his family to Belfast so he could keep an eye on the new mill he and his brother were building near the Dufferin rock quarry. That in itself must have required a considerable amount of adjustment to children used to an outdoor existence. Yet presumably it must also have had its compensations because Amy left no record of disappointment at the move. The excitement of the new mill, together with living in a city that offered new and different activities, probably helped them to accept the challenge of their new situation.

A much more serious threat to Amy's happiness had arisen before the move to Belfast. She had been sent off to spend three years as a boarder at a Wesleyan Methodist school at Harrogate. Perhaps it made Amy wish that she had been kinder and more tolerant to the succession of governesses who had tried to educate the Carmichael children! No doubt her mother and father sent her to Yorkshire firmly believing that they were taking this step in her best interests, but Amy would never have made this choice herself.

After the freedom and companionship of brothers and sisters in a lovely Irish setting, the restrictions and petty rules of her boarding school proved irksome, and she gained the reputation among her contemporaries as "a rather wild Irish girl . . . and something of a rebel."

However, as always, small children brought out the best in her, and a school friend reported that she was always very gentle and loving both with the little girls at school and also with her friends' brothers and sisters when she stayed there on vacations.

Poor Amy must have felt like a caged bird in her new surroundings. Indeed, she used just this expression about herself when she wrote a poem on the subject years later:

A little wild-bird child,
But lately caught and nowise tame,
And all unreconciled
To cages and to careful bars.

In her adult life, she acknowledged that the sight of three growing things had helped to cheer her up in her first acute bout of homesickness: a saucer of moss, a tall white lily in a pot in the dining room, and a box of chrysanthemums her mother sent from the small greenhouse at home.

Throughout her life, flowers would always be important to Amy. Years later in India when she saw a likeness between the tiny, innocent children snared in the evil Temple practices and the beautiful lotus flowers growing around a roadside pool, she would fondly call them "my lotus buds."

Try as she would to stay out of mischief, Amy often found herself getting into scrapes at school. She said little about those times in later years, merely admitting honestly, "If I told you much it would not help you, for I was not at all what I want you to be." By the time she was fourteen, she had developed into a natural ringleader among the girls. She saw all too little of her brother at a boys' school nearby so had to rely on the companionship of her schoolmates.

So often for Amy good intentions backfired. Her friends urged her to ask the principal, Miss Kay, if the older girls could stay up to see the famous comet in 1882. Faced with a certain refusal, Amy behaved in the only way a girl of spirit could: she kept the girls awake by pulling a thread tied around their big toes. Unfortunately, when they crept upstairs to the attic to view it from the skylight, they found the principal and her staff had already anticipated them and were up there watching the skies! Much to her relief, Amy wasn't expelled; she knew that would have upset her parents terribly, and she would have hated to have been forced to leave under a cloud.

But the years at Harrogate were far from wasted. Toward the end, something very important and significant happened that made a profound difference to the rest of Amy's life. The newly formed CSSM (Children's Special Service Mission), held a crusade at Harrogate. Mr. Edwin Arrowsmith, one of the founders, was addressing the young audience on this occasion.

Amy, of course, was no stranger to Bible stories. As a tiny child she had sat cradled on her mother's lap while she sang to Amy and told her about the love of the Lord Jesus. Often when she used to lie alone in her nursery bed with the light turned low she would pray to her Heavenly Father, "Please come and sit with me." So from her earliest days she had felt surrounded by the love of God, and this gave her an immeasurable sense of security.

However, after his talk, Mr. Arrowsmith asked the children to sing, "Jesus loves me, this I know," and then sit quietly for a few minutes. During this short time for reflection, it dawned upon Amy that it was *her* responsibility to accept God's invitation. Then and there she invited Jesus to take control of her life. This step was taken in childlike simplicity, but as she progressed in her Christian life she began to understand more of the tremendous sacrifice that Christ had made on behalf of all mankind, and she never entertained any doubts about her future salvation. Christ had done it all. Probably because she passed through this experience as a child, she was always anxious to hand on the gospel message to whatever children came into her care, without pressuring them, realizing the value of this vital episode in her life.

It was just as well that Amy had made this important decision at this stage because more changes were looming on the horizon for her, mostly unpleasant, which would demand all her courage and resolution to endure. It is true that the first alteration in her circumstances could have been a welcome one for her, because she was taken away from school in Harrogate and brought home for good. However relieved Amy might be to finish her education in Ireland, attending classes in music, painting and singing at school in Belfast, the fact remained that the move was due to a decline in their family fortunes. Boarding-school fees became out of the question, and Amy's brothers returned home also for the same reason.

The more mature Amy now enjoyed an even closer relationship with her father, who led a very busy life on top of his business obligations, often speaking at functions and helping his wife to entertain the many visitors who were invited to their home. But their happy family life was abruptly terminated by David Carmichael's serious illness. The strain of financial affairs had already taken its toll on him. When a friend to whom he had lent several thousand pounds found himself unable to repay, David refused to demand his money back. No doubt weakened by the mounting pressure, he eventually contracted a severe chill that led to double pneumonia. David died at the early age of fifty-four on April 12, 1885. Amy must have been thankful for the happy companionship she had experienced in these last few months, reading to him on his sickbed.

Amy, as the oldest in the family, found herself the close confidante of her mother, shouldering fresh burdens and responsibilities now that their family had been deprived of its breadwinner. Later, her brothers and sisters would pay tribute to her care and attention for them over these next few years. However engrossed she was with her duties for the immediate family, she never became narrow in her outlook but was always stirred by the sick or underprivileged. The doctrine of socialism attracted her when she first came in contact with it, but it was the idealized form in its purest concept that drew her admiration. Later she was to realize that it could be fallible if practiced with the wrong motives.

Quite often in the lives of famous people there comes, completely unexpectedly in the most mundane of circumstances, a flash of revelation which seals that person's destiny for ever. Some, though not all, might describe it as a call from God, but all would agree that it makes clear the direction in which their future service lies. It happened to Florence Nightingale, Edith Cavell, Mother Teresa, and many other devoted servants of God.

Amy related her own revelation in her book *Gold Cord* and clearly felt it was of great significance to her. She and her brothers and sisters were returning home from church one rather dreary Sunday morning together with their mother, when they met a poor old woman, weighed down with a heavy burden. Impulsively, they relieved her of her bundle and offered her a pair of strong arms to help her on her way. Suddenly the Carmichael youngsters realized to their embarrassment that it meant facing all the respectable, well-dressed people following behind them from the service. Perhaps a few eyebrows were raised at these youthful Good Samaritans.

Whatever the reason, they felt hot and uncomfortable and acutely aware of the old woman's shabby attire. Let Amy tell the most personal, intimate part in her own words, because it had such a profound influence on the rest of her life: "But just as we passed a fountain . . . this mighty phrase was suddenly flashed . . . through the gray drizzle: 'Gold, silver, precious stones, wood, hay, stubble—every man's work shall be made manifest; for the day shall declare it . . . and the fire shall try every man's work of what sort it is. If any man's work abide—' (1 Cor. 3:12). I turned to see the voice that spoke to me . . . The blinding flash had come and gone; the ordinary was all about us. We went on. I said nothing to anyone, but I knew that something had happened that had changed life's values. Nothing could ever matter again but the things that were eternal."

A moment's vision? Perhaps so, but its impact lasted throughout the years. One of Amy's brothers left it on record that Amy "shut herself in her room that afternoon, talked to God and settled once and for all the pattern of her future life." Her sister also spoke of "various good works" done by Amy, two remarkable testimonies in themselves. Rarely is a servant of God recognized and respected by those nearest and dearest. The Lord Jesus himself knew this well: "A prophet is not without honor, save in his own country, and in his own house" (Matt. 13:57). Yet Amy's own work and witness must have been so unself-conscious, so unself-seeking that her family saw the purity of her motives. Here was no ego trip, no desire to acquire a reputation as pious and religious but just a natural, warm urge to show the love of the Lord Jesus in a practical way to fellow human beings.

These "good works" took several forms. On Sunday afternoons she would sometimes knock on doors in the streets surrounding College Gardens and bring home children for a children's meeting, with tea provided afterwards by Mrs. Carmichael. Amy and Eleanor Montgomery used to teach a group of boys at night school on Monday evenings, rounding off with a "good-night service." Eleanor's father, Henry, belonged to the Belfast City Mission, and he often took Amy around the poorest and most sordid streets of the city on Saturday evenings. It must have been a startling revelation to a girl reared in a secure Christian home.

The "Morning Watch" was another of Amy's own innovations. All members, including two of her brothers, promised, and even signed a pledge card, to spend time daily in prayer and Bible-reading. Then they would meet on Saturdays to discuss their progress—or confess their lack of it—to the other members. But they didn't turn out to be dull and solemn occasions; Amy saw to it that the discussions were lively and everyone came away happy. She spent time also at the local YWCA helping in a positive but self-effacing manner.

Respectable people appeared quite shocked when Amy persuaded the minister of the Presbyterian church where the Carmichael family attended to allow a class of "Shawlies" to meet every Sunday morning in the church hall. These folks were mill-girls who covered their heads with shawls instead of conventional, Victorian hats, and who therefore were held in suspicion and were almost outcasts of polite society. Amy saw and recognized their need, persuading one of her brothers who was an apprentice engineer to fill in for her the sordid details of their often depraved circumstances. All this surprised a great many people, as did her tramping up and down streets normally regarded as too dangerous for delicate-minded young females from sheltered homes. Nevertheless, this did not worry Amy in the least. "Perhaps my mother believed in an angel guard" was her only recorded comment.

This "determination to get down to the root of things" as her brother stated, was to stand her in good stead many years later when she found it necessary to penetrate haunts of dire evil and degradation in India to rescue her beloved children. No experience, however unhappy and unnerving, was wasted in her opinion—her banishment to boarding school, her beloved father's untimely death, and her encounters with squalor, poverty, and sin in the Belfast slums all prepared her for what she would have to face. "The things which happened to me have fallen out for the furtherance of the gospel" (Phil. 1:12) became her philosophy of life, just as they were for the apostle Paul who wrote these words in a Roman jail.

3

Working for the Lord

*P*erhaps most people might consider that one direct message from God would have been sufficient to launch Amy on her life of service. Certainly it contained great import for her and changed her outlook. Amy was never again the same high-spirited teenager after that incident. Still full of fun and happiness, she nevertheless found a new purpose and urgency in spreading the gospel message among the deprived and neglected members of society. She recognized that the revelation she was given while helping to carry the old woman's bundle was the first milestone in her spiritual journey. "From this pool flowed the stream that is the story," she wrote later in *Gold Cord*, the book that describes her work in India.

Yet God must have seen a need to give her another personal touch to confirm His calling. On a visit to Scotland in 1881, she went with a friend to a convention held in a hall in Glasgow. Although anxious to hear direct guidance from the Lord, Amy felt unmoved through the two addresses.

Later, in *Edges of His Ways*, Amy amplified that incident. "Some time after I heard, and for the first time understood and believed, that we could be kept from falling, I was at a big meeting in Scotland. . . . I was near the back and could not catch a word except this word *all*. He read 2 Corinthians 9:8 and I have never forgotten that *all*. 'God is able to make all grace abound toward you; that you, always having all sufficiency in all things, may abound to every good work.' "

The opening words of the final prayer, "O Lord, we know You are able to keep us from falling," finally inspired her, just as if they were meant for her alone. She kept repeating them to herself throughout the day to savor their depth and meaning. From that time onward, Amy became convinced that the former social frivolities, though pleasant and harmless, were not sufficient for her.

Grant that I may reach them,
Grant that I may teach them,
Loving them as Thou dost love,
O give Thy love to me.

Amy wrote these lines much later on in her life, but they serve to show her attitude toward needy people from her teenage years. Her work with the "Shawlies" developed fast. Amy found herself in the situation where she required a permanent hall to seat at least five hundred. She possessed little money of her own and her mother's slender resources as a widow were stretched to the uttermost to cover the family's basic expenses. Yet Amy felt certain that it would be wrong to make an appeal for money. God would provide it through sympathetic Christians.

One day, while Amy was out making formal calls with her mother, some interested Christians asked the two ladies about this possible building. They in turn put her in touch with a Miss Kate Mitchell who offered to donate the whole sum. A mill owner whom Amy interviewed granted them a piece of land in a prime position in the city for a very nominal rent. And so the hall was erected and dedicated by Dr. Park, Amy's minister.

Again it wasn't the speaker's words that burned deep into Amy's soul but the words printed on a long banner just above the platform. "That in all things He may have the preeminence" (Col. 1:18) was to prove the basis of Amy's complete ministry. Nothing, absolutely nothing, of any worth would be achieved unless God was put first in every transaction.

Two students from the Moody Bible Institute led the opening crusade, which saw many people converted. Although often in urgent need of money, Amy stuck by her principle of praying for it rather than making the matter known. "God shall supply all your need, according to His riches in Christ Jesus" (Phil. 4:10) was the text in which she firmly believed. She was not alone in this. Other well-known Christians like Hudson Taylor, George

Muller, and C. T. Studd followed this method, and
God never let them down either in their missionary
or orphanage work. The other rule to which Amy
adhered was not to recruit any assistants to help
at The Welcome, as the hall was called, unless they
were completely in sympathy with her aims and
methods. It would only have caused trouble and
dissension otherwise.

A printed card advertising the various meetings planned for the week showed a formidable list
of events requiring an intimidating amount of hard
work and organization. It would have been easy to
take advantage of any offers of help with such a
tiring program every day of the week, but Amy
stuck to her guns and only accepted dedicated
Christians. After a while she gathered around her
a loyal band of assistants who lightened her load
and made it easier to hand over the work when her
circumstances changed drastically later on. Miss
Mitchell herself, who had put up the original purchase money for the hall, took charge of the place,
thus relieving Amy of anxiety on that score when
she and her family left dear, familiar Ireland for
the uncertain joys of living in dirty, smoke-grimed,
industrial Manchester.

In 1888 when Amy was just twenty years old,
the remaining money left by her father was lost in
a financial crash. Characteristically, Mrs. Carmichael showed no signs of panic when confronted
by such a serious misfortune but knelt down with
her seven children and prayed over the problem.
Amy, with her usual energy and vigor, came up

with some practical suggestions to alleviate the immediate difficulties. Over the next few years, her two older brothers emigrated to America and later the other two to Canada and South Africa.

In 1889, Mrs. Carmichael left Belfast with two daughters for England. It was by special invitation of a close Christian friend that Mrs. Carmichael became the superintendent of a rescue home, and Amy started a work for factory girls similar to The Welcome in Belfast. Conditions were hardly ideal. Amy rented a room near the hall where she spent her days. It was absolutely filthy. Amy wrote about "the most loathly sort of insect which . . . would crawl through the thin walls from our next door neighbor's house into ours." She ate sparingly, rarely taking the time to cook a meal, and drove herself hard as she worked in the slums.

It was a dangerous area in which to live, and Amy wrote an account of how she was mobbed by hoodlums on the way to visit her mother at her cottage in the country. A friendly woman ran out of her house and dragged Amy to safety, but it was nevertheless an unwelcome experience, taking its toll on Amy together with illness, poor diet, and overwork. Eventually it all became too great a strain on her, and she reluctantly had to give up her efforts in Manchester, which opened up a completely new phase of her life.

It must have been an anxious time for Amy when she was forced to abandon the work in which she had been so wholeheartedly involved.

But through it she was learning the inscrutable ways of God.

God moves in a mysterious way
His wonders to perform.

Years later, in her book of meditations, *Edges of His Ways*, she quoted the text from Exodus 13:21: " 'The Lord went before them . . .' We may have a timetable, even so, we face the Unknown. We may not know what a day may bring forth, but if we are following our Leader we know that we shall be led."

Amy's affairs took an unexpected but not unpleasant turn. In the story of the Trapp family, depicted in *The Sound of Music*, a heartening phrase can be found, "God never shuts a door but He opens a window." He already had the window ajar for Amy to enter. Earlier in 1887, Amy had first come into contact with Robert Wilson of Broughton Grange, Cumberland, when he was acting as chairman to a convention in Belfast. He called at her grandmother's house for a discussion, chatting for quite a while and then praying before he left.

"We did not expect to see Mr. Wilson again," wrote Amy afterwards, "but somehow we became friends and when he returned home he wrote to us and we wrote to him."

Several times Amy and her sisters and younger brothers visited him in his home, and it was through him that she first attended the well-known Keswick Convention. This had been founded in 1875 as a continuous week of meetings "for the deepening of the spiritual life." Many important speakers were invited to take part, and a great number of people were helped to rededicate their lives, take up some form of Christian service in Britain, or go overseas as missionaries.

To the Carmichael family, Robert Wilson eventually became known as "DOM," the Dear Old Man. He evoked their love and sympathy as his wife had died at the same time as their father, David, and he had lost his only daughter even earlier. When in 1890 he asked Mrs. Carmichael to spare Amy to be his companion, it couldn't have been an altogether welcome suggestion. She and Amy enjoyed a very close relationship with each other. She generously allowed the arrangement, however, and Amy commented later, "I knew afterward it had not been easy . . . and yet looking back I can see that it fitted into the Plan . . . certain great lessons not learned yet had to be learned."

Like many others on the Christian journey through life, Amy realized that a major obstacle that she might have preferred to avoid was turning out to be a stepping-stone leading her in the right direction. Similarly, Paul wouldn't have chosen to become a prisoner in a Roman jail, but he could rejoice that through those circumstances many people in that city were coming into contact with him and becoming Christians. "Man proposes but God disposes."

Amy, left to herself, would probably have made a different series of decisions, but in the end she could see God's overruling guidance in the matter.

No doubt, at first she was thankful to relax and regain her strength following her strenuous efforts in Manchester. She found sufficient work to occupy her in entertaining the many important speakers who came to Broughton. As chairman of the Keswick Convention, Mr. Wilson was involved with many men of God whom Amy found it a privilege to meet.

The DOM had been born into a Quaker family, but later Mr. Wilson's sympathies widened to embrace other denominations, and he felt quite free to worship in an Anglican church and to help run a Baptist Sunday school. This taught Amy a valuable lesson, "to drop labels and to think only of the one invisible Church, to which all who truly love the Lord belong."

It wasn't all a bed of roses, though. Two of Robert's sons, still bachelors, lived at home and naturally resented Amy's presence in the house, although they appreciated her care of their father. There must have been times when she felt in an awkward situation, but she took refuge in various activities in the village, such as Scripture Union meetings held in the Mission Hall.

Saturday afternoons were reserved for a girls' Bible class. Amy, with vivid memories of her own happy childhood, made sure that the children played games before the class. Afterward they were given refreshments and taken around the garden to view the pets. This realism stayed with Amy all her life and influenced her attitude toward her many children in India. In planning programs, she always sought to obtain the right balance so that the children grew up to be happy and natural, not insufferable little prigs.

All this experience would prove an asset in later years as would the friendships she made after she left Ireland. In Manchester, she became acquainted with Ella Crossley and Mary Hatch, who later became staunch supporters of the work in India. Then when living in Cumberland, she joined Hannah Govan of the Faith Mission, touring villages around the Clyde in an evangelistic tour in 1890. It was about this time too that she wrote her first published article. Although Amy and her brothers and sisters had occasionally put together a family magazine, she had no confidence in her ability to write. At that stage, no one could possibly have foreseen the long list of thirty-nine books that would appear under her name.

It looked as though Amy had not only recovered physically from the exhaustion that caused her work in Manchester to come to an abrupt stop, but had even started to explore new avenues of service. Her younger brothers and sisters were finding their niches in society, some in different countries, and her mother was happily settled not too far away from her. She found emotional satisfaction in caring for Robert Wilson, taking the place of his daughter who had died years earlier. Wilson himself was sixty-six years of age and happily involved in Christian duties. He and Amy enjoyed a good rapport. She was extremely useful to him as a hostess and companion but at the same time felt free to pursue various projects of her own. Although she still met with some opposition from the DOM's two sons, it was not intolerable, and no doubt she hoped that time would heal the difficulties. There seemed no reason why she should not continue in that way of life for many years to come.

And yet Amy would never be content with the easy way out. It was she who wrote:

> *From silken self, O Captain, free*
> *Thy soldier who would follow Thee.*
> *From subtle love of softening things,*
> *From easy choices, weakenings . . .*
> *Let me not sink to be a clod:*
> *Make me Thy fuel, Flame of God.*

4

Japan and Ceylon

A my used to look back with pleasure—and with wonder—at the times when God had spoken to her clearly and with a particular message. This phenomenon was to happen once more on January 13, 1892, when Amy, shut cozily within her own room, snow piling up outside the Grange during a winter's evening, decided to have a quiet time for reflection. There was no angelic vision, no flashing lights or melodic choirs, but just a simple, heartfelt conviction that the Lord was saying, "Go ye—to those dying in the dark—50,000 of them every day, while we at home live in the midst of blazing light," as she wrote to her mother the next day.

"I had thought that the plan was for me to stay with the DOM till he went to heaven," she confessed years later. That did not seem an unpleasant prospect for her, though still only a young woman. She had learned to love and respect him. Again and again in her writings appear little glimpses of him, dear memories of the times he had proved a spiritual help to her. In *Thou Givest ... They Gather*, for example, she recollected, "Week by week, always on Saturday evening as a preparation for the worship of Sunday, the dear old man who was a father to me used to pray, 'We thank Thee, O Savior, for the much incense of Thy merits,' and the phrase sank deep into my mind, and all these years stayed with me." It was just as if Robert Wilson was saying that all the goodness, truth and beauty of the person of the Lord Jesus Christ was going up to heaven to delight His Father like a cloud of sweet-smelling incense.

Later on in the same book Amy discussed the agony of decision-making. "There are times when we wish that an angel from Heaven would come and tell us what we ought to do. . . . Am I in perplexity, not knowing which of two paths is the one for me? . . . Sometimes there is pain, personal pain. Christ is not concerned to make things easy for us. But peace is the certain portion of the child of God who is in the will of God."

That peace didn't come automatically at once to Amy. She passed through deep heart-searching, as she told her mother in a letter the next day. First she weighed the practical considerations of her far from robust health and the deep need her mother and Wilson had of her.

"Mother, I feel as if I had been stabbing someone I loved . . . and through all the keen sharp pain which has come since Wednesday, the certainty that it was His voice I heard has never wavered; though all my heart has shrunk from what it means, though I seem torn in two, and just feel one big ache all over, yet the certainty is there—He said to me 'Go,' and I answered, 'Yes, Lord.' I never knew what it would cost."

How could her widowed mother with some of her children already scattered far and wide reply? When Charles Studd, the great missionary pioneer and founder of the Worldwide Evangelization Crusade, confessed to his mother that he had received a call from God to take the gospel to heathens in far-off China, she was aghast and distraught, causing Charles great agony of decision, although eventually he sailed with her promise of support.

This was not to be Amy's problem. Her mother replied almost immediately. After quoting a poem, Mrs. Carmichael wrote, "Yes, dearest Amy, He has lent you to me all these years. . . . So, darling, when He asks you now to go away from within my reach, can I say nay? No, no, Amy, He is yours—you are His—to take you where He pleases and to use you as He pleases, I can trust you to Him and I do." In her thoughtful way she went on to say, "For dear Mr. Wilson I feel so much, perhaps more than for myself, but God has his happiness in His keeping."

Fortunately for history, not only these two letters were preserved but the DOM's as well. Unselfishly, he appeared more concerned about Mrs. Carmichael's loss than his own sense of deprivation. "I know something of what it must cost you, but am sure He who calls for this, will more than fill the void caused, by His own love flowing in."

Letters traveled from mother to daughter for several days. Amy was concerned with the practical, financial details of her mother's life and also distressed by the reaction of her aunts and Mr. Wilson's two sons. She was misunderstood by both families involved. They thought her heartless and callous to abandon her mother and her "adopted" father. "He will be dead before you are through the Mediterranean."

Strangely enough, although quite certain of her call, Amy was unsure of her destination. She mentioned Ceylon frequently as a possibility in earnest conversations with the DOM and also with her mother when she stayed with her for a long visit. After being present at Keswick for the convention that year, details became a little clearer. She was to be the first missionary supported by the Keswick Missionary Committee and she offered her services to the China Inland Mission whose General Director, Hudson Taylor, was a personal friend of the DOM.

Amy even got to the stage of packing her trunks for the long sea voyage when her plans were suddenly halted by the CIM doctor who refused to pass Amy as medically fit for China. Mr. Wilson was overjoyed at this reprieve and delighted again in Amy's companionship as she helped him with his affairs. It looked as though she was settling down into her former comfortable way of life. On the surface, everything appeared as before. Only

Amy was aware that it could not go on indefinitely. "Always the thought was with me, 'This is not your rest.' I knew I must go, but where?"

Exactly a year after her "distinct call from God," Amy began to consider the possibility of Japan. Robert Wilson, as soon as he knew, gallantly offered to contact the Rev. Barclay F. Buxton, who had already been working in Matsuye for a couple of years. No doubt it cost the DOM a good deal emotionally when he would much rather have kept Amy by his side.

Without waiting for a reply from Mr. Buxton, Amy decided to set out on her journey having been in touch with the China Inland Mission. She arranged to sail on the SS *Valetta* on March 3 in company with three other women missionaries. She went through the double agony of parting first with her mother at Manchester and then the DOM at Tilbury. Even fifty-two years later in 1945 she could recall the tension. "It was such a rending thing that I never wanted to repeat it." The parting was protracted at London with a farewell meeting to go through first.

On the first leg of the journey to Colombo, Amy enjoyed the voyage in spite of a spell of rough weather and even ran a daily Bible class for anyone who cared to attend. The next boat, which she boarded at Colombo for Shanghai, was less luxurious and was infested with rats and insects. As usual, Amy found a rewarding compensation; the Captain was converted to Christianity. "I am so happy about the Captain," she wrote in a letter home, "my heart sings every time I think of him."

Much to her relief, letters of confirmation and welcome from the Buxtons awaited her at Shanghai. After addressing a few gatherings of missionaries there, she pressed on to Japan, arriving at Shimonoseki in a violent storm with floods of rain. Because of the weather, no one was there to meet her and she couldn't communicate with the Japanese. Fortunately, Amy's sense of humor didn't desert her—she could usually see the funny side of life in the most bizarre situations—"I laughed till I was positively aching." In the end she was helped by a friendly American. Her meeting with Barclay Buxton on May 1 was all that could be desired. She always revered him as a genuine man of God.

It is difficult to guess why Amy set off for Japan after having been turned down as medically unfit by the China Inland Mission, without waiting for a reply from Barclay Buxton. Was she acting impetuously or as the result of some firm inner conviction? Although at the beginning of her period of service she couldn't possibly have known she would spend so short a time there, she immediately became involved in evangelism, fitting in language study whenever she could between trips.

Later in India, she would reverse this procedure with recruits so they possessed a working knowledge of the language before they attempted to travel around spreading the gospel. What she lacked in fluency in Japanese, however, she made up in caring love for her converts. Fairly soon after her arrival she adopted Japanese dress to identify more closely with them. Later, she published a book about her experiences in Japan, so a clear picture emerges of her life-style and work-pattern in that country. With supreme honesty, Amy described not only success stories but sometimes incidents that showed that everything did not proceed smoothly and automatically.

> *O for a passionate passion for souls,*
> *O for a pity that yearns!*
> *O for the love that loves unto death,*
> *O for the fire that burns!*

These four lines came from a poem penned by Amy in Japan. During that period it seems probable that she sorted out priorities in her life. Very likely someone cared deeply for her and she had to weigh the various claims upon her. God's demands won; from that time personal relationships had to take second place to her burning "passion for souls." It can't have been an easy decision for her to take and must not be dismissed glibly. However ardent the missionary, human ties are always very precious, and this step represented a costly sacrifice on Amy's part. A favorite quotation of hers was from John Buchan (quoted in *Thou Givest . . . They Gather*) and it indicates her underlying philosophy. "Have no fear. . . . You have chosen the roughest road, but it goes straight to the hilltops."

Amy rejoiced as God gave her her first converts. She did not take it as a personal triumph but gave Him the glory and acknowledged the prayer support both of her English and Japanese colleagues. All this activity was not without stress. Phrases in her letters home must have concerned her family: "Bad neuralgia" and "acute neuralgia" were frequently mentioned in early 1894. Finally she warned her mother, "The doctor wants me to go to China for a complete change this summer."

It cost her a good deal to say goodbye to her friends in Matsuye. Some of them even suggested Amy should proceed straight home, but she was reluctant to do anything so drastic after only fifteen months in Japan. She must have felt as confused and anxious at the extraordinary turn of events as her relations and friends in England when she confided in them that God was planning for her to work next in Ceylon! "What will people say? How strange it will look! Nobody will understand!"

There had been suggestions of a period of convalescence at Cheefo on the North China coast, but that scheme gradually faded out. The cost of traveling to Colombo was considerably less, and many of Amy's friends felt that a long sea voyage might be more beneficial to her health. Fifteen months in Japan fell far short of her original expectations. Yet it had proved an immensely fruitful time. She had led many people to the Lord, particularly in Hirose where there had been a good deal of blessing. Amy always remembered that and wrote later, "Often in India I thought of Hirose, and longed with a great longing to have an Indian Hirose. But it was never given. Perhaps it is that the Lord does not repeat himself."

Disappointed as she might be, Amy showed determination in tackling her future responsibilities in spite of poor health. She sailed on July 28, but she had already started to come to grips with the Singhalese language, which she would need in her new situation. Again she had set out without receiving a reply from the band of Christians in Ceylon who belonged to the Heneratgoda Village Mission, but thankfully she received a warm welcome on arrival.

She threw herself wholeheartedly into evangelism with local workers, many of them descendants of the Dutch settlers. However, unsettling letters kept arriving from Japan from friends who sadly missed her and communications from home warning her not to join any mission in Ceylon. Amy hated to feel misunderstood, but she stood firm on one point and agreed not to become a permanent member of the Mission. "It may be He has only sent me here as a stopgap."

She enjoyed a temporary improvement in her health, but the doctor was worried about her long-term prospects. Friends advised a complete rest once more, but the prospect of a long voyage home was an intimidating one and Amy decided to carry on. Finally, the matter was taken out of her hands as she received the news that Robert Wilson had suffered a severe stroke. Within an hour Amy set off for home assisted by kind friends.

The journey must have seemed like a bad dream to Amy, who wrote in the margin of her Daily Light, ". . . in much fear, ill and alone." Later in Paris she confessed, "I must have been ill, for there are long, blank spaces," but from other observations, she obviously felt the Lord was still in control.

Her mother met her in London, but Amy wasn't sufficiently well to travel straight to Cumberland. Kind friends from Keswick days took care of her until she had recovered enough to complete her journey. She finally arrived at Broughton Grange in time for Christmas 1894, twenty-seven years old, with a large question mark hanging over her future.

5

India at Last

January must have held many memories for Amy with her call to the mission field in 1892 and her specific direction to Japan in 1893. January 1895 brought with it nothing dramatic, nor did the months that followed. It gave Amy time to recover, and Robert Wilson also, but both were too honest to imagine they could settle down into the old routine. Although events had taken an unpredictable turn, Amy never doubted her original call. But she needed a miracle to set out on her travels again because any doctors consulted refused to recommend her for service in a tropical country.

As usual, Amy was not content to live the life of a semi-invalid but made use of the opportunity to put together her first book for publication, *From Sunrise Land*, containing her letters from Japan. Amy was critical of it afterwards, but it did draw attention to the needs of that faraway country and make people aware of the work going on there.

A letter from a friend in Bangalore, South India, stirred Amy's interest in that part of the world when she remarked, almost casually, that the climate might suit Amy as it was so healthy. This caused Amy to set the wheels in motion again. Although not wanting too easy a situation, she was forced to be realistic about her health problems as she could not afford another breakdown.

She was first interviewed by the leaders of the Church of England Zenana Missionary Society in London and then accepted by them at Keswick in July. She addressed the missionary meeting in the tent and left a profound impression on her hearers. Although she had worried in the past, "What will people say?" following her departure from Japan, there was no further need for anxiety. She was appraised for her own true worth and certainly not misunderstood.

Again Amy had to face up to the emotional strain of a double parting, first from her mother and sisters on September 30, and then from the DOM again on October 11. If Amy left England with any misgivings, she left no record of such feelings. Certainly she couldn't have foretold at that stage that she would remain in that country for over half a century.

Her first three weeks were spent in Madras at the home of the CMS Secretary, Mr. Arden. His younger daughter, Maud, became a dear friend and ally and a valued fellow worker later on.

Amy's personal charisma must have been powerful; without conscious effort on her part she continually attracted people to herself who remained loyal and helpful to her in her efforts as a missionary to rescue young Indian children.

It was an unfortunate and inauspicious beginning to her stay in Bangalore that she arrived on December 4 suffering from dengue fever. Although carefully nursed through the attack, it left her feeling low and depressed for quite a while. Still the old irrepressible Amy bubbled up occasionally, as when, for instance, she raced the Residency carriage on her pony, Madcap. It was hardly a customary activity for single missionary ladies, but from time to time Amy defied convention. It helped her to identify with the children she cared for later on. "I felt exactly as you feel sometimes, only more so," she revealed to them.

Although thankful to be back in harness again, Amy felt far from happy in Bangalore. She didn't altogether see eye-to-eye with some of her fellow missionaries and their methods of evangelism. True, they were kindly disposed to her, but they already had a full workload and she found no close friend in whom she could confide and share interests. The experience, however unpleasant, wasn't altogether wasted because it helped Amy to sympathize with similarly placed young missionary recruits later on.

Someone with less determination than Amy might have given up at this stage. She had launched herself straightaway into a concentrated study of Urdu, no easy task, only to be switched over to Tamil so that she could become the official hospital evangelist. But it wasn't Amy's way to back out of a difficult situation. In *Edges of His Ways* she quoted an example of someone she admired. " 'She has neither rusted out, nor burned out. She is burning still.' I read that in an Australian magazine and I prayed that it might be true of each one of us. We want most earnestly not to rust out, we would gladly be burned out."

So Amy went on burning herself out in language study and her colleagues worried about her health. Was this to be just one more apparent failure? There was no indication at this stage how successful her ministry in India would prove in the long term. On the positive side, during a stay at Ootacamund, a hill resort, Amy met Walker of Tinnevelly. Although she wasn't particularly impressed by him at first, she accepted his offer to be her Tamil teacher and decided to leave Bangalore. Eventually he would become her loyal friend and adviser, a pillar of strength in a strange land.

The move to Tinnevelly was almost thwarted. Amy was out driving with a friend who just missed plunging into a ditch in the moonlight. Life would never be easy for her. She herself possessed a strong feeling that ". . . a Force—powerful but not all-powerful—was resisting my going south." A favorite sentence of hers quoted in one of her books expressed her attitude to difficulties: "Life's not a level or a smooth road; but it's a blessing to scale the hills and trudge over the stones with a good heart, and I think one sometimes does one's best work on the uphill bits, though one may not know it."

The language lessons forged a close bond between Mr. Walker and Amy. Both he and his wife learned to appreciate her increasingly, and by agreement with the Bangalore missionaries, she was released to work with the Walkers in their visits to towns and villages previously unreached by the Christian gospel. It proved to be an intimidating task. Few really dedicated Christians could be found in the area, although there was a host of nominal church attenders. The Walkers and Amy moved into a bungalow at Pannaivilai in July 1897.

From this time on, Amy adopted Indian dress (although it met with some adverse comment from some of the European missionaries), and she started to gather around her a group of young converts to form her Women's Band, aptly named The Starry Cluster by the Indians. One such was Sellamutthu, who remained Amy's loyal friend and companion for forty-three years. Another, of whom much is written in Amy's book, was Ponnammal, a young Christian widow who had been greatly helped by Mr. Walker's teaching. She showed her worth initially as a Sunday School teacher, but eventually they managed to wring consent from her father-in-law to allow her to join Amy's Band. This he did very reluctantly

because he had been using Ponnammal as an un-
paid servant in his own house.

Amy was soon to learn what treasures she had
gathered around her. The work was extremely arduous (although they did stay around Pannaivilai in the hottest weather). Their daily routine
was to travel out to a village by bullock cart, visit
homes to talk to women and children and then
observe a short rest or siesta after the meal before
they set out again. Occasionally they were joined
by the Men's Band and quite often spoke in the
marketplaces or streets to any people who were
prepared to stop and listen. Apart from the work
being hard in itself, the native women must have
found it difficult to face up to criticism by other
nationals. It required a great deal of courage to
lead such a public life when Indian women were
usually regarded as their husbands' chattels and
merely fit for mundane household duties.

Amy was overjoyed when her helpers quietly
returned to her the extra payment she gave them
for every night spent away from home! "We don't
need it. Please keep it to meet other expenses
involved in the work," they urged her. A costly
sacrifice—they owned very little—and completely spontaneous and unprompted.

Amy was soon to rejoice again in an even cost-
lier sacrifice, which she herself had not dared to
suggest. Wearing jewelry was common practice
in that area and denoted a woman's status. If married, it showed too her husband's situation in society. Strangely enough, it started with a young

husband telling his wife, who was working with the Band, that such a display of wealth was unsuitable for the purpose. This incident spoke to other members, who gladly stripped off their own nose rings, earrings, bracelets, and necklaces.

Ponnammal's relatives and others in the church became extremely angry. Members of the Band, however, were quietly convinced that their action had been pleasing to the Lord. And there was one practical spin-off; up to that time women had avoided traveling by night because of the fear of attacks by robbers. Now that members of the Band had voluntarily given up wearing their jewels, that danger no longer existed.

Had the evangelists kept a low profile in their village work, people might have turned a blind eye to their activities. But the Amy who wrote "Make me Thy fuel, Flame of God" and wanted to "burn out rather than rust out" was not content with anything less than total conversions. She with her Band and Mr. Walker with his helpers made a concentrated attack on the stronghold of the Enemy. Two girls at different times escaped from their guardians and relatives to join Amy for teaching and protection. Amy was allowed to keep them with her at Ooty. Another young girl, Arulai, listening to an open-air preaching, saw Amy in her Indian dress and was immediately attracted to her. It wasn't as simple as with the two previous girls, Jewel of Victory and Jewel of Life, who were old enough to choose for themselves. Arulai, only eleven, was held in close custody by her relatives. It took many months of suffering and intense prayer before Arulai was at last allowed to join Amy's family.

Even at that stage, it was still impossible to predict how this work would develop and grow. At the encouragement of her friends she wrote an account of the beginnings of her ministry with young people. The Committee at home would have preferred it to be glossed over a little with the difficulties understated. Amy, however, entitled her book *Things as They Are*, and that is how it appeared in print in 1903.

Difficulties didn't discourage Amy. They represented a challenge to her but only served to emphasize God's almighty power in every situation. A favorite poem that displayed her philosophy clearly was written out in *Thou Givest . . . They Gather*.

> *He has for thee*
> *A light for every shadow,*
> *A plan for each tomorrow,*
> *A key for every problem,*
> *A balm for every sorrow.*

It didn't mean that Amy never became downhearted or despondent, but she possessed inner resources and had Someone to whom she could turn in any emergency, however grave.

A significant change occurred at that time when the Band moved, initially only for a short while, from Pannaivilai to Dohnavur. No one imagined then that the name of this small Indian village would become internationally famous. To them it was just a convenient center for evangelizing.

Amy was laying solid foundations during her first few years in India. She had gathered around her some faithful friends who worked closely in harmony with her. The language problem was becoming less acute as Amy practiced it constantly, and with improved communication there came a closer understanding with the people who so desperately needed her help. Her health was causing her less anxiety, and after the relatively short stays in Japan and Ceylon, she was enjoying a period of continuity in her Christian service. At last she could see how that "call" was being answered.

But Amy's life was not, at last, absolutely free from frustration and interruption. No missionary ever experiences completely smooth sailing. Although quite convinced that she was in the place where God would have her, she was always aware of tugs in the opposite direction. Naturally she must have missed her mother, and she felt a deep concern for the DOM, who had suffered another slight stroke. Should she return home to look after him? If so, what would happen to her Indian converts in the meantime?

Faced with a difficult decision, Amy was misunderstood by many who thought her place was at the DOM's side. If she did return to England, it would be all the more agonizing to leave a failing old man again. He himself finally gave his blessing to her to carry on with the work at Dohn-avur, but it still did not decrease his longing for her presence and support. The DOM lingered on until 1905 and it cost her much anxiety. Often she fell prone to self-questioning, tormenting herself about his weakness and frailty, but the greater need lay in her adopted country with the children she had fought for so hard.

6

A Growing Community

*I*n her book *Gold Cord*, Amy acknowledged her debt to the DOM. Pasted on the flyleaf of his old Bible, which Amy always kept with her after his death, were the significant words, "Follow no voice, not mine or any other which is not His. My soul, wait thou only upon God, for my expectation is from Him." Letters from Robert Wilson followed Amy to China, Japan, and India and helped to mold the fellowship at Dohnavur.

Why the title *Gold Cord*? Amy explained that friends kept asking for something to link together stories that had already been written. "What holds you together?" they asked. "A gold cord" was the immediate answer.

The first Temple child who escaped was brought to the bungalow at Pannaivilai where the team had only just returned that very day from a year spent in Dohnavur and the neighboring area. Preena had already escaped once before, but her mother gave her back to the Temple women and her childish hands were branded with hot irons as a punishment. For a while Preena remained on the Temple grounds, but the prospect of "being married to the god" became a terrifying nightmare, although she was too young to understand exactly what was involved.

Amy's enemies used to describe her as the "child-catching Missie Ammal" to scare children and their parents, but Preena had become so desperate it appeared the lesser of two evils. When Amy first saw her she sat Preena on her lap and kissed her "like a mother." It was love at first sight and in spite of the Temple women arriving to try to take possession of her again, Preena was adamant and flatly refused to follow them. Amy became much closer than a natural relative to her, for had not Preena's own mother given her back into the hands of evil men and women who sought to pervert her?

God's timing was absolutely perfect—but then He always works "in the fullness of time" (Gal. 4:4). Preena only summoned up enough courage to escape on the very day the Starry Cluster came back to their bungalow. God was protecting this child. She might never have reached safety and security had Amy and her helpers still remained at Dohnavur. The date of Preena's arrival held such significance for the fellowship at Dohnavur (for it represented a tremendous breakthrough) that later on it became a custom for the whole Family to meet together for prayer on the sixth day of the month to dedicate to the Lord children who had come to them rescued from grave moral danger and also to pray for the many who still remained in great peril in the various Temple towns in southern India.

The wisdom of Amy wearing Indian dress can clearly be seen as this young girl quickly identified with someone whose appearance looked comforting and reassuring. How much more the wisdom of God is evident in giving Amy the brown eyes she first despised! Amy appeared a natural "mother figure" to these distressed children, abandoned by their own parents. The pattern of Amy's life also began to unfold as her peculiar ministry to the Temple children developed. The years she had spent as the eldest of a large family helping her younger brothers and sisters, and the times she had trained youngsters in her Scripture Union classes at Broughton Grange bore rich fruit. She possessed a deep understanding of and a warm empathy with needy children of all ages. Amy admitted in her book *Ponnammal* that "there had been a very empty corner somewhere in me that the work had never filled." Now the Lord was to grant her a profound emotional satisfaction in rescuing these children and bringing them up in the Dohnavur Family.

It grieved her intensely as she unraveled the sordid story of what it meant for them to be "married to a god." Some of the details were published in *Lotus Buds* and other books, although she left out many of the more harrowing stories.

Children might be handed over to the Temple women as a thank offering or for several other reasons. Occasionally a poor woman might dedicate her child because she could not afford to keep her, or an abandoned child might be picked up by them. Both members of the mission and the government were shocked by these startling revelations. Largely through Amy's efforts it became illegal to "marry" a child to a "god," but this did not stop the practice altogether; it merely drove some of the operations undercover.

This, of course, did not happen in one single transaction. It took Amy three years to discover the source from where the Temple children were derived. It involved many secret journeys and clandestine conversations, which often placed the Starry Cluster in grave danger.

If the progress of the work had been recorded on a graph, it would have shown troughs and peaks. In 1901, five boys were baptized in the water near Dohnavur, but within weeks two of them died, possibly of cholera. Among the triumphs there were disappointments as when, for instance, a child was snatched from Amy's care and never seen again. Arulai was baptized, and then some time later her life was almost lost when she fell a victim to typhoid and pneumonia.

One thing became clearly apparent: Amy needed to devote herself almost entirely to the care of her "family." For their sake she settled at Dohnavur, which lay in a sheltered position quite a distance from the main road. At first rather unattractive with a sparse covering of grass, over the years it gradually took on a new appearance with a succession of buildings wreathed by a wealth of flowering creepers.

From that time onward her primary objective was to devote her energies to saving little ones— girls at first and then later boys as well—although she was persuaded once to accompany the Walkers to an annual convention at Travancore in 1902 and leave her "family" in the care of other trusted helpers. The rapturous welcome she received from her children on her return more than compensated for the pain of her absence.

Ella Crossley and Mary Hatch arrived for a visit in the autumn of 1903, and shortly afterward Mr. and Mrs. Walker left on furlough.

Mr. Walker, whose wife had been dangerously ill, had had to leave Amy with the heavy responsibility of her own growing family and his converted boys as well, but Amy had no qualms. By summer of the next year she was responsible for seven members of the Starry Cluster and seventeen children—and still they kept coming. Soon the very first Temple baby was presented to her, only thirteen days old, and was called Amethyst; she was later joined by Sapphire.

About this time Amy felt it was high time to start building a nursery; completely unsolicited gifts started to come in for that purpose. The year of the Walkers' absence passed quickly because of the new expansion program. Amy was delighted to greet Mr. Walker on his return, although sad that his wife was not sufficiently well to travel with her husband. But an unexpected treat was the arrival of Mrs. Carmichael with Mr. Walker.

Amy's mother drank in the new sights and scenes, vividly describing them in her letters home to friends: "I am greatly struck by the simple child-like faith of some of these dear convert girls. . . . I often wish my friends at home could see these dear children . . . they are so bright and affectionate." Her one regret was that she could not communicate with them in Tamil, but she enjoyed their company, nevertheless, and they managed to teach each other a few words.

As a mother she was also concerned about her daughter's health. Although pleased that Amy appeared stronger than in her early missionary years, she deplored the fact that often she was up half the night when the little ones fell sick. And the babies too gave no cause for complaisance. Several thrived, but they lost Amethyst and another baby. Feeding was the big problem. At that stage foster mothers refused to cooperate in wet-nursing the children. Probably they were afraid of incurring the displeasure of the Temple authorities, but some of the babies could not take reconstituted dried milk.

It wasn't easy for Amy to lose any of her little ones after she had rescued them from danger and learned to love them. "There is one puzzle which comes to all thinking people when a little child is taken to be with the Lord . . . sometimes He asks for the loan of one of these precious gifts. He does not tell us why He asks for it . . . and we know that He will return what we lent Him when we see Him in the morning" (*Thou Givest . . . They Gather*). Unfortunately, it was a situation that Amy had to face many times over the years, and in spite of her faith it never became any easier.

Mrs. Carmichael was able to share her daughter's joys and sorrows while she was staying at Dohnavur. It also gave her a very real insight into the workings of the fellowship, which she could never have gleaned from letters alone. No one had set about forming a constitution or drawing up rules and regulations. They just learned to live together in a loving relationship with a common purpose. The need of the thousands of Temple children in great moral danger was sufficient motivation. But one golden rule always held: Under no circumstances was anyone to make an open appeal for money.

No hierarchy of jobs existed. Amy herself would get up at night to soothe any sick child. By day she could be found dusting, sweeping, and gardening along with the others. Naturally, a great deal of the organization and written work fell on her shoulders, but she refused to stay deskbound, out of touch with reality. She possessed the maternal instincts of a true mother.

During October 1905 the Christians at Dohnavur experienced a very real outpouring of the Holy Spirit, which made a marked difference to the whole neighborhood. Around that same time they received news of Robert Wilson's death. Mrs. Carmichael was still in India and was able to comfort Amy in a special way, having known him well and Amy's relationship with him. No one else there could have consoled her so sympathetically.

On her return to England, Mrs. Carmichael was able to make a much more informed contribution to the missionary newsletter she and one of her other daughters sent out. Failures and successes were faithfully recorded. Urgent prayer requests were included as well as thanksgiving for answered prayer. A trained nursery helper was desperately needed. Ponnammal had been left in charge of the tiny infants at Neyyoor the previous year. This arrangement was made so that the little ones could be within easy reach of the London Missionary Society's hospital. Amy missed them while they were away from Dohnavur, but it seemed the most sensible policy. She possessed supreme confidence in Ponnammal, who always slept with the frailest baby in her own room and gave of herself unsparingly in her service for the children.

During a serious outbreak of dysentery at Neyyoor, Amy wrote of her: "Weak and frail herself she kept all going quietly, and in an orderly fashion, and she inspired her workers with her own beautiful courage." Ten little ones died before the epidemic petered out. It almost seemed as though the enemy of souls was going all out to attack those who had snatched these precious children from his evil clutches.

Lessons were learned from the outbreak. More nurseries were urgently needed with isolation wards to keep the sick children from contact with others. Trained medical help was also required to deal with such outbreaks. Mabel Wade, a trained nurse from Yorkshire, joined the staff in November 1907. She immediately fit in perfectly, finding Dohnavur her spiritual home, although the work proved difficult at first as there was no doctor with whom she could consult. Mabel had total responsibility for the health of the Dohnavur family.

Thankfully, Ponnammal and the babies came back during the next year to be permanently re-housed in the new accommodation. Great was the noise and great the rejoicing!

There was always room for dedicated Christian women to help with the daily care of the children, but Amy expected people of the same caliber as Ponnammal and Sellamutthu, and they were few and far between. Some joined the staff and left again fairly quickly. Others started cautiously with a few natural misgivings only to become wholly involved in a very short time. Expecting a missionary home to be steeped in a dull, solemn atmosphere, they were agreeably surprised to find Dohnavur very relaxed—a place of great happiness and joy.

It was hard, demanding, selfless work, consuming one's whole time and energies, but those who stayed the course claimed it was also utterly rewarding. Amy wrote as the first generation of children was growing up, "those unseen guardians of their childhood must . . . feel repaid for their vigils by little white hammocks, and for many a walk across to our rooms at night to call us to come. And we, too, have been a thousandfold repaid for anything we ever did" (*Gold Cord*).

For some time there had existed a need for a teacher for the growing children. A highly qualified one came only to leave for England after a relatively short stay due to poor health. Everyone who could had to make their contribution to the children's schooling. Amy described herself as "Jack of all trades, master of none." She had originally traveled to India as an evangelist, yet her life work appeared to be looking after the bodies and minds of small children, a task for which she sometimes felt ill-equipped. Yet the Lord enabled her, and wisdom and intuition came with the years.

7

Mixed Fortunes

*P*eople often have a distorted impression of children being cared away from their own natural home surroundings. Dohnavur wasn't like an institution at all. Each and every child was made to feel welcome and treated as an individual, in spite of the large numbers. Their personal and emotional needs were carefully considered. In her book *Kohila*, Amy recorded an account of a child who joined the family and stayed on as a helper: "For as we do not often know birthdays, we keep instead the anniversary of the day a child comes to us." So each child had a "Coming Day" celebration when she was given a party and presents, then prayed with on her own.

Amy, or Amma as the children called her (the Tamil name for mother), was always accessible to her young charges. She came under a certain amount of criticism from people who misunderstood her role. Surely she had been sent out to take the gospel to the heathen, and instead she busied herself with small boys and girls most of the day! "Inasmuch as you have done it to the least of these My little ones, you have done it unto Me" (Matt. 25:40) was her philosophy.

Dohnavur never possessed great financial reserves. Amy observed, "Those were years of rigid economies, for though we were never burdened about funds, we thought in terms of pence, not shillings, much less pounds . . . no one knew that we were at times almost in straits. They only knew that all our needs were supplied." Nevertheless, Amy tried to keep the buildings as attractive as possible, knowing it was important for the children to see beauty in their lives.

Many times events placed her under a great strain, as when, for instance, her children were made the subjects of lawsuits to try to wrest them away from her. Amy admitted in *Gold Cord*, "All through those years of beginnings we had lived with a menace in our ears. It was like living within sound of the growls and rumblings of an approaching storm. At last, in 1910 and 1911, the storm broke upon us and we were plunged into a welter of troubles in the law courts." In all these affairs she leaned heavily on Mr. Walker for his guidance, spirituality, and expertise.

The long story of Muttammal, who came under her protection for a while and then was wrested from her by wicked relatives, is a complete story in itself. After years of lawyers and court appearances, the girl was finally smuggled away from India by a friend of Amy's and taken to live with missionaries in China in order to be removed from grave personal danger. The outcome proved to be a happy one. Eventually she married one of the young Christian men from the Family on Colombo and then returned with him to live in Dohnavur. A fairy-tale ending to all her wanderings—or rather the ending of faith after almost impossible odds stacked against her. Needless to say there was great celebration, but the long, drawn-out struggle took its toll on Amy's health and proved a severe mental strain. Nevertheless, her faith never faltered under fire, in spite of harrowing court appearances, and in a miraculous way the money came in to pay the legal expenses just in the nick of time.

Amy was buoyed up by the everyday happiness of living with children who had been snatched from the powers of darkness and whose lives had been dramatically changed. Yet being involved with so many young ones meant she was vulnerable. In August 1912, Lulla, a little Brahman child, passed away suddenly before medical help could arrive. Only six days later, a telegram arrived with news of the completely unexpected death of Mr. Walker, who had left a few days earlier to take several meetings in Masulipatam.

Naturally, Amy grieved deeply over the loss of both the child and Mr. Walker, a pillar of strength to her since the early days of setting up the fellowship. In her sorrow, Amy—unselfish as usual—had sympathy to spare for Ponnammal, whose heart ached over the death of her young charge, and also for poor Mrs. Walker, away from the events in England, and not in a very robust state of health herself. But if troubles didn't come singly, neither did the compensations. God held reserves in hand for just such a crisis as this. Two sisters, Edith and Agnes Naish, who had been intending to become involved in village evangelization, traveled straight to Dohnavur to offer their services on hearing of the bereavement. Agnes, with many years teaching experience behind her, took over the task of supervising the children's education, which lifted a great load from Amy's shoulders.

A young Christian man, Arul Dasan, who had previously worked with Mr. Walker, offered to supervise the building work. By 1913 the Family had doubled from the seventy members belonging to it in 1906, so there was a continuous program of extensions to meet with the demand, which really needed a man to oversee the whole effort. In addition, he helped with the writing in Tamil and English.

But with the lightening of the load came other pressures. Ponnammal, one of the mainstays of the children's work, fell ill with cancer. Amy nursed her through two operations at the Salvation Army Hospital at Nagercoil. Meanwhile, Arulai left to cope at Dohnavur in their absence and was faced with seventy of her babies being affected by a malaria epidemic. Fortunately, none of them died, but some who recovered with complications that were difficult to treat were brought to Nagercoil for further treatment. With one group came a letter from Arulai, "Are you tasting the sweetness of this time? I am." What a comfort this proved to Amy who was torn in two directions during that period, longing to support Arulai in her struggle against the illness and yet knowing that her place was with Ponnammal in her suffering.

Ponnammal died on August 26, 1915, and Amy recorded her life of service in a book, *Ponnammal, Her Story*. She was a helper who could never be completely replaced.

Other loyal supporters arrived over a period of time to help with the education of the children. At one stage, Amy was forced to make a difficult decision between carrying on as before or receiving a very welcome grant from the state, which meant that in addition she had to admit non-Christian teachers on the staff and also accept some of their choice of textbooks. The offer of money was tempting, but it meant a compromise for which Amy was not prepared. Years later she could see the rightness of her choice when books were chosen that were displeasing to Christian teachers and parents. God had clearly guided.

A few days before Ponnammal's death, Mrs. Carmichael also died, and the home in Wimbledon that had been an unofficial headquarters for the Dohnavur work closed down when Amy's sister moved out. Later, Mrs. Irene Streeter, who had paid two visits to Dohnavur, agreed to be the official representative in England.

People might imagine that Dohnavur, tucked

away in an isolated part of India, would remain untouched by the First World War, which was being waged largely in Europe. True, all the Family was free from immediate physical danger, but finances dipped to an alarming low. The value of the pound began to fall and by 1919 it realized less than half its pre-war value. "And yet we were enabled to go on," wrote Amy in *Gold Cord*. ". . . never once was a child left unsaved or unfed because we had no money or feared that we should not have enough in the future." Even extensions to the nurseries were planned and executed, although there were no great reserves in the bank.

In 1915 Amy herself was feeling the strain. Her diary gives a glimpse of her state of mind. "Lord, teach me how to conquer pain . . . when my day's work is done, take me straight Home. Do not let me be ill and a burden or anxiety to anyone." It was just as well then she could not see the manner of her own passing and the many years of weakness and pain she would be called upon to suffer. She could not have foretold what a blessing her last long illness would bring to others.

When Bishop Frank Houghton set about writing Amy's official biography, he was confronted with gaps in the records. In her self-effacing way, Amy had torn up diaries and notebooks, but later on she became reconciled to the possibility that some account would eventually be written. Glimpses of her personal diary are all the more precious for not being complete and letting readers share her innermost thoughts and feelings.

Money—or lack of it—proved a frequent source of comment. "Mail in today, and £50 from a friend . . . Took letter up to field where children were weeding, and we all praised God standing in shadow of cactus hedge." Amy's children would learn about the Lord and His marvelous ways not from formal sermons but firsthand, from on-the-spot situations. It became all the more real to them because their dear Amma shared her hopes and fears with them, and also God's solutions to her many problems.

Amy wrote three books over this period—*Nor Scrip*, *Tables in the Wilderness*, and *Meal in a Barrel*—to show how God faithfully supported them through every crisis. Amy took some persuading at first for she was never keen on personal publicity, but she did want to share the story of God's goodness to Dohnavur with others. Always Amy refused to accept support from one person to one particular child; whatever money came in went straight to the general fund.

It wasn't by chance that the Carmichael family lost most of their money and learned to live in greatly reduced circumstances while Amy was only a teenager. Through this apparent misfortune, Amy learned firsthand how to rely on God, and Him alone, for all her needs and how to wisely use the money that came in. This stood her in good stead later on when she had to balance the budget for her large and growing Indian family.

She also wrote the *Life of Walker of Tinnevelly*, which for some time she held back, fearing that people in England would be too engrossed with war news to want to read about a relatively unknown village in India. To Amy's surprise, when finally published, the book met with an amazing success. Although cut off from quick, direct communication with Europe during both World Wars, Amy was distressed over the atrocities and sufferings she heard about. Involved as she was with her Temple children, she still had sympathy to spare for other poor unfortunate human beings.

People who visited Dohnavur began to recognize her uniqueness. A Keswick speaker, Dr. Inwood, left this record: "The two days spent here have no parallel in my experience. Everything in this work has the touch of God so naturally upon it that I lived in one unbroken act of wonder and worship and adoration . . ."

Other people outside Christian circles were beginning to appreciate Amy's contribution to the welfare of Indian children. In January 1919, she received a telegram from the Governor of Madras, congratulating her because her name had been included on the Royal Birthday Honors List. Her award was the Kaisar-i-Hind Medal. Amy's first reaction was to wonder if she could refuse it, but her friends talked her out of that, saying it might appear ungracious to the Crown. Yet nobody could persuade her to go in person to accept the medal. Who could have foreseen in November 1895, when Amy first set foot in India, that in just about a quarter of a century this unknown missionary would become almost a household word?

In the early days, a visit to Ooty in the hills brought a refreshing change for Amy, her helpers, and the youngsters, anxious to get away from the heat of the plain. Later, her journeys there almost ceased. As the number of children grew, it had become increasingly expensive to pay for accommodation, and it was a long trek from Dohnavur. As a compromise, Amy made do with an empty Forest Department bungalow in Sengelteri, in the mountains above Dohnavur. Being cool and near a river for bathing, it served her purpose for a number of years.

Yet always in the back of her mind lurked the idea of a permanent place that would belong to them alone and be large enough for their purpose. After many fruitless visits, they were led to a place called the Grey Jungle, which immediately appealed to Amy. The asking price was £100 for 37 acres of hillside. True to form, in spite of her natural enthusiasm, Amy prayed for a sign before she proceeded. The next day she opened a letter from a lawyer in Ireland telling her she had been left £100 in a friend's will. Confirmation indeed!

It would be a satisfying, fairy-tale ending to say that the work went just as smoothly as the purchase. On the contrary, heavy rains, unsatisfactory workmen, and difficulties on the site brought delay after delay. The children themselves worked valiantly carrying loads. Amy cheered everyone on, even when one corner of the veranda fell down. Two of the Hindu workmen attending evening meetings asked for baptism and the ceremony took place in the pool below the Forest House. That alone made all the hard work and effort more than worthwhile.

Amy made sure all the children learned to swim as a safety measure because of the depth of the pool. It was she who organized picnics for the children's delight. The house provided hot weather retreats for countless workers and children over the years and was the scene that brought much inspiration to Amy when writing her books and poems.

8

The Family Grows

And can it be He walks these woods
These paths that we have swept?
Then may my heart with all her moods
Be holier kept.

It was just as well that Amy had established this
peaceful retreat. On the surface it might have
seemed that the worst crises had already been met.
Amy had collected around her a dedicated team of
loyal helpers; many little girls had been snatched
from the evil clutches of the Temple priests and
were florishing in Dohnavur; the Indian government had recognized Amy's services to the nation;
she had become an established, respected figure.
Then late one evening just before January 1918, a
new force to be reckoned with arrived at Dohnavur. A weary woman holding a tiny bundle
stepped out of the bullock cart, and Amy took the
child from her arms. Faithful Mabel carried the

child off to the nursery and then raced back to announce, "It's a boy!" Arul had entered the Family.

For Amy it was the culmination of seven years anticipation. Perhaps people imagined that she had decided to concentrate her efforts on saving only little girls. It was not a conscious decision, just that there had been too many obstacles in the way at first and Amy already had her hands very full. But part of her was still very much aware of the problems of the boys. She had noticed rows of little boys from eight to ten years old playing instruments in Temple courts. Quite often, like the girls, they were adopted as babies by the Temple women and then trained to act with the dramatic companies or in the temples. Scouts were always on the look out for particularly talented and attractive young boys.

Amy knew full well that far from providing a career for these children, it meant that it was impossible for them to lead wholesome and pure lives in that environment. They were young and defenseless and could not protect themselves from their evil masters. The first time Amy felt concerned and burdened about the boys, Mr. Walker was away on furlough. Wisely, she kept the matter to herself until he returned.

There were some very obvious obstacles. Amy and her team were already stretched to the uttermost. In those days it wasn't "done" to keep boys and girls together in the same compound. So after they were segregated, male helpers would be required—and where would they come from?

She had shared the project with Mr. Walker
when he returned, but his advice was to wait, although he could see the need. He felt Amy was
already fully committed and she reluctantly was
forced to agree. After 1911 came Mr. Walker's own
death and Ponnammal's long illness and subse-
quent death, so the subject was shelved for the
time being but never totally dismissed.

The Dohnavur family was well aware of what
was going on in Amy's mind—she had shared it
with them—but there was a general feeling that the
Lord would send them a doctor before the boys
could be admitted. Boys needed more delicate
handling than girls and the help of a doctor could
prove vital. In the end, Arul arrived before any
plans had been made.

There was plenty of room to have boys' nurseries constructed in a field alongside the girls'
compound, so Amy had plans drawn up and
prayed to the Lord for £100 to start the work. We
have to remember that in India in those days it
would have been considered very improper to
keep boys and girls together, so Amy had to make
quite sure that the conditions were such that they
would attract the right sort of children in need and
yet arouse no public criticism. She had only a short
wait for the first sum of money. It didn't come di-
rectly to her but as a legacy to a fellow worker who
gladly passed it on without a moment's hesitation.

Once the building project was under way, Amy
longed for other boys to join the family! By this

time she had a network of friends throughout South India whose hearts God had stirred to keep a look out for children at risk. But of course they couldn't just snatch such children and run off to Dohnavur. Often it required great patience, tact, and even cunning. Amy could not afford to flout the law of the land and often she had to bide her time, even though her heart burned to provide shelter for a little one.

As with the girls, God in His wisdom did not allow a sudden influx of boy babies. Amy could not have coped with too many at once. Her first doctor—a lady—arrived much to everyone's rejoicing yet, soon had to return home on account of her health. They must have wondered what God had ultimately in mind for them.

In *Gold Cord* Amy gave a vivid description of how she managed to worm her way into a building in Madras where boys were being trained for the theater. "Twenty-five . . . lads of all ages between six and seven and seventeen and eighteen, beautiful boys . . . crowded round, friendly and lovable and keen to make the most of this welcome interruption to an apparently strictly enforced routine. Suddenly the outer door was flung open and an angry man rushed in upon us like a whirlwind. 'Off to your lessons, boys!' "

Amy commented in her diary, "O to save these, to perish for their saving. Lord show the way." Arul delighted in Amy taking him on her lap on his Coming Day and saying to him, "You are my very first son." It was this deep sincere love for each child that drew them first to her and then to the Lord. Amy had time for each one and treated each as an individual. Within six months a brother came to join Arul, but another eight years elapsed before Godfrey Webb-Peploe arrived to take over the boys' work, which involved some seventy or eighty little fellows by that time. As with the girls' leaders, Amy inflexibly set the highest standards for her male helpers, but then these people had to take the place of parents to these children who had been snatched from the grossest forms of evil. It was through their leaders they would first hear about the Lord Jesus Christ, so first impressions were tremendously important.

Amy already had the support of seven Indian girls who had grouped themselves into a "Sisterhood of Common Life" in March 1916. Its name was derived from the Brotherhood of Common Life founded by Gerard Grote of Holland in 1380. They were laymen, taking no monastic vows but going out into the community each day after worship and returning at night. Amy introduced the Sisterhood to the writings of outstanding mystics. The sisters voluntarily chose to remain single, and several groups were formed over the years. But very few male workers felt they were called to be celibate, so no Brotherhood was created. Each sister tried to live as closely as possible to the teachings of our Lord, remembering that He humbly girded himself with a towel at the Last Supper so He could serve His disciples in love. "We are trusted to spread the spirit of love," wrote Amy. It was a disciplined and demanding pathway but infused with joy and happiness. It certainly wasn't meant to be dull and negative.

Some people misunderstood Amy as a result of this, believing that she took a strong stand against marriage. This was far from the truth. Whenever possible, she prepared her girls for Christian marriage as long as a suitable partner could be found for them and integrated many couples into the Dohnavur work and also outside. But she felt strongly there was a need for a few dedicated people who would be totally committed to the care of the children without any outside distractions.

All these activities gave great pleasure to Amy, but they also took their toll. No one could give so much of herself to others without feeling grief and pain on their behalf. Like her royal Master, she proved compassionate and caring, but it hurt deeply.

> *No wound? no scar?*
> *Yet, as the Master shall the servant be,*
> *And pierced are the feet that follow Me;*
> *But thine are whole: can he have followed far*
> *Who has no wound nor scar?*

Toward the end of 1921 came another curious incident completely divorced from Amy's usual activities with children. From time to time, Amy heard stories from the coolies that carried her chair, of Jambulingam, an outlaw, who called himself Red Tiger and lived in the forest rather like Robin Hood, robbing the rich to succor the poor.

This proved a challenge to Amy. "I wonder if I could arrange a meeting and tell him about the Savior?" she deliberated.

Incredibly, this happened. Jambulingam had spied on her with his men while she was supervising some building work in the Grey Jungle. After several days he waylaid her and, at Amy's request, poured out his sad story while Amy shared her tea with him and his followers. Although completely innocent, he had fled in great fear to Penang when falsely accused. Returning to find out about his wife and children, he found the police terrifying his wife. He fled again and his wife died of shock. Knowing there was no hope of real justice being done, he remained an outlaw in the mountain, giving his gains to the impoverished peasants.

Amy promised to take care of his three children, and he in return said he would never use a gun except to defend himself. She also pleaded with him to give himself up but he refused, yet they had a few short minutes together for Amy to tell Jambulingam about the Savior and pray with him.

Only just in time! Within five days he and his friend Kasi were caught, tortured, and sent to a hospital while still under guard. Amy visited him and left him a Bible to read. After having a dream, Amy asked him if he would like to be baptized. The ceremony took place, even with the priest she had dreamed was officiating—an amazing coincidence.

Visits ceased after that, except for a Tamil clergyman who instructed them once a week. Then his trial dragged on. Eventually, Jambulingam, Kasi, and two others managed to escape from the jail. Only Jambulingam and Kasi kept together in the forest. The other two deserted them when they knew they were no longer prepared to rob and steal as before.

Amy sent message after message to plead with them to give themselves up to the authorities again. False rumors went flying around, although she herself felt confident that they had kept their word. Finally, staining her face and arms and wrapping herself in a dark sari, she allowed herself to be taken to their hideout in the jungle. Jambulingam swore to Amy he had not been robbing, but he was too frightened to place himself at the mercy of the government officials. They prayed and repeated Scripture passages together, including the 23rd Psalm.

Next day they fell into an ambush. Running to get away, Kasi slipped and was shot. Jambulingam waited for his friend, threw down his gun, and then was cruelly attacked and shot by the police. Again, false rumors flew around for a long time. In the end, Amy wrote the full story in *Raj, Brigand Chief*. She herself had been the subject of much criticism because she defended these men verbally. In the book she disclosed how others had become Christians because of the testimony of the two men. She had never sent them any supplies apart from Christian literature. Although her sympathies went out to them, she did not allow her

judgment to be clouded; technically they were acting outside the law. Yet she longed and fought for
the law to be changed so that unfortunate people
would not be falsely accused and persecuted like
Jambulingam.

Father, hear us, we are praying,
Hear the words our hearts are saying,
We are praying for our children.
Keep them from the powers of evil,
From the secret, hidden peril . . .

Amy could have been so deluged with her ad-
ministrative duties that she would have had no
time for the little ones as individuals. Wasn't it
enough to rescue them from grave and moral evil,
feed, clothe, and educate them? Not nearly
enough, would have been Amy's reply.

Coming from a happy family background herself, she recognized the importance of loving,
warm relationships. These Indian children no
longer belonged to their own families, so Amy felt
she had to supply that love and security they
would have otherwise missed. She made up funny
songs, poems, and stories for them, kissed them
good night as long as possible, and made a great
fuss over them on their Coming Day. She preferred
not to dwell on their unhappy lives before they
arrived at Dohnavur. Often she prayed to the Lord
to ask Him to remove painful incidents from their
memories.

There were times, however, when Amy found
it necessary to punish her charges. However much

she disliked it, she had no intention of spoiling them. The punishment was always swift and just, tailored to fit the crime. Then afterward Amy never bore a grudge. As far as she was concerned, the matter had been dealt with and then forgotten.

The standard of education had to be updated also to keep abreast of the times. Schools and hospitals run by the fellowship had to be staffed with those who had gained the necessary qualifications, and rightly so. Amy accepted this without question, but always her primary motive was to bring up boys and girls to be good soldiers of the Lord Jesus Christ. Time and results have vindicated her aim.

9

Stepping Stones and Stumbling Blocks

*T*he decade between 1920 and 1930 saw a vast expansion. Workers pressed forward with the main concern of rescuing boys and girls from danger so new nurseries were constantly being added. At the same time, the task of proclaiming the gospel in the surrounding villages proceeded, with the Starry Cluster circulating in the area. Some of the older Dohnavur girls accompanied them for training.

The reputation of Dohnavur spread and attracted many new workers from a variety of countries. Amy worried about the increase in numbers but soon found that the newcomers blended in happily with the original staff because they all had the same aims and objectives. That does not mean to say that mistakes were never made or the wrong people appointed. Ripples appeared on the surface sometimes. Everyone had to work hard at maintaining an atmosphere of mutual love and trust. After all, however dedicated, they were only human. Amy wrote of her apprehension as the work grew; she could see possible difficulties. Then later she penned the lovely phrase, ". . . that strange lovely knitting of hearts together, that instant understanding that needs no words."

Halfway through the decade came a period of great importance. There appeared to be two outstanding needs in the way of buildings. One was a House of Prayer and the other a hospital. Of the two, the hospital seemed the more pressing, but Amy had a sixth sense that she should concentrate on the House of Prayer. A few small money gifts for her birthday plus a contribution from some missionaries in Algiers confirmed her opinion. The architect and the builder of the Chapel of the Women's Christian College in Madras together with their wives visited Dohnavur for Christmas. Amy was thrilled—another of God's important coincidences—and the work began. The House of Prayer was dedicated by Bishop Tubbs in November 1927. The building was starkly simple but truly impressive.

Another significant visit in 1925 was the arrival of Godfrey Webb-Peploe. He and Amy established instant rapport; they were kindred spirits. She sensed in him a sympathetic and like-minded worker, but unfortunately he was traveling to China as a missionary with the Children's Special Service Mission, so there was no chance of Amy prevailing on him to stop at Dohnavur. She certainly wouldn't have dreamed of doing so, but he made a deep and lasting impression on her. It wasn't just a social call. Godfrey arrived with an older friend, R. T. Archibald, to conduct a mission in Dohnavur, which proved very profitable. Godfrey and Amy "rejoiced together," to use her words, before he traveled on.

Various other stresses assailed Amy that year, although it is not always possible to gain a completely clear picture of events from her diary. She was suffering some anxiety over a new worker who had joined the team. For weeks she agonized over the decision. No one was ever accepted lightly; much prayer was expended on every fresh volunteer. All through the months from May to November the inner conflict waged. Finally, the worker had to go. It would have been possible for Amy to tear these pages out of her diary so that no one outside the fellowship knew about the incident, but that wasn't Amy's way. She never built a cult around her, or considered herself anything more than a fallible human in God's service.

Over the same period, Dr. Marguerite Stewart, one of the "New Seven" valued workers, fell dangerously ill and had to be taken to Neyyoor for several operations. For quite a while she hovered between life and death with Amy praying constantly for her. Eventually, Marguerite recovered, much to everyone's joy and relief, but it meant the loss of another new worker at Dohnavur that they could ill afford.

Yet, every year had its compensations. Like ordinary families, the Dohnavur family experienced ups and downs. In July, a Syrian Christian who was an official of the Travancore Forestry Department, was instrumental in offering them sixty acres of land on a rocky hillside. Amy acknowledged, "We signed the check on our knees," but it proved a good investment in the years ahead. This was no ordinary site; it overlooked the Pilgrim's Way to Cape Comorin and was given the name "Three Pavilions." In past centuries the three kings of Travancore, Madura, and Tanjore used to meet there in council. The views were magnificent; winds and storms swept through the area.

Amy paid three pounds an acre for the land and immediately met with opposition from the priests in a small, nearby roadside temple. Eventually when good rains in the first year brought the promise of ample crops, the local landowners welcomed the Christians, thinking the rain was a good omen and the old head priest became a friend to the members of the fellowship.

A house for the workers was constructed there and a nursery school for the more delicate children who were either physically or slightly mentally handicapped and could not fit into ordinary school life in Dohnavur. The invigorating climate worked wonders, and the children enjoyed the spaciousness and tranquility. As always, Amy paid many visits there while the work was in progress and gathered the workmen together for prayer. But it was not until 1936 that Amy welcomed two new permanent members of the staff who would take over the responsibility of running Three Pavilions, Vivien Tomkins and Jean Ewing.

Through the same Syrian Christian, Amy also bought a small plot of ground near the sea, fifteen miles from Three Pavilions. She called the house that she had built on the spot "Joppa," and it proved a refreshing place of rest and relaxation for tired Dohnavur workers. She hoped it would become a place of witness for pilgrims at the very tip of India.

Although Amy was beginning to have inner qualms about who would succeed her when she was no longer able to carry on the work, we still see glimpses of the happy, adventurous child of the Millisle days. She provided the House in the Forest, Three Pavilions, and Joppa for her family's rest and relaxation. She made up stories for them, played games with them, and taught them to swim in the Forest pool. Right up to 1931 she was riding around the compound on a tricycle, but sometimes the children became too enthusiastic in pushing her around sharp corners and a few spills ensued. The nickname of Musal Ammal (the Hare) stuck with her because she liked to do things at full speed. It is amazing when one thinks back over her long period of weakness and ill-health in her late teenage years. The friend who wrote advising Amy that the climate was healthy in Bangalore little knew what great results would come from her suggestion!

By 1925, Amy and Mabel Wade realized it was

foolish to carry on as missionaries with the Church of England Zenana Missionary Society. Not that they had a difference of opinion, but the Dohnavur work had run independently for some years, and many of the workers there had no association with the CEZ. Amy had always maintained that she alone would be responsible for the Dohnavur finances, but somehow a verbal agreement wasn't satisfactory. It was necessary to make a watertight legal arrangement because of the tenure of land and property. The Church Missionary Society generously gave them some of the old buildings and adjacent land they had been using, and by 1927 the Dohnavur Fellowship was officially registered with the following constitution:

"To save children in moral danger; to train them to serve others; to succor the desolate and the suffering; to do anything that may be shown to be the will of our Heavenly Father, in order to make His love known, especially to the people of India."

Although formal language was used for the constitution, it was made abundantly clear that the Lord Jesus Christ was the supreme authority, and everyone had to bow to His will. All nationalities were welcome as long as they shared the same ideals. It was particularly important for members to be fully integrated and completely at home because, although large, the Dohnavur work was a single unit. Other missionary societies could change people around to different centers if there was a personality clash, but there was no possibility for that at Dohnavur. Although Amy tried to give a true picture in her books, some readers were misled, believing Dohnavur was an ideal environment in which everyone lived in peace and harmony.

As the personnel increased, the local pastor asked Amy to arrange her own church services for the children because of overcrowding. Eventually, members of the fellowship took the services, but there was no deliberate breakaway movement from the Church of South India.

Occasionally members of the staff left the work at Dohnavur but, even then they took up service again in other parts of the world. Sometimes it was a question of mistaken guidance, but Amy was always reluctant to write them off as a failure, and she always rejoiced if the Lord could make use of them elsewhere. Most, however, took root there and happily followed Amy as their leader.

Three primary questions were constantly on Amy's mind. Who would come forward to lead the boys' side of the work? In view of the pressing need for a hospital, who could be relied on to see all of that program through? And finally, now that Amy had nearly reached her sixtieth birthday, whom would the Lord send to take over the torch from her? Amy kept on praying with no firm assurance. Amy wrote in her book of meditations *Thou Givest . . . They Gather*, ". . . from the midst of frustrations in Central Africa, Fred Arnot, who was the Livingstone of those regions, wrote, 'I am learning never to be disappointed, but to praise.' " Naturally she was crestfallen that Godfrey Webb-Peploe was already committed to China when in her eyes he appeared the ideal man to fill the gap at Dohnavur, but she still kept on praising. She kept on working, too, not complaining about the tools God was providing just because some of her dreams were not being realized. Later in the same book comes a significant little verse that seems to encapsulate her philosophy in just four lines:

To each is given a bag of tools,
An hourglass, and a book of rules;
And each must build ere his work be done,
A stumbling block or a stepping stone.

"We cannot build both ... we must choose which we will build. Once built it stands; we cannot pull it down and begin over again. God help us all to build stepping stones."

A final quote from the book also appears very relevant to the situation as Amy found it at that time. "It has been said, 'What we see as problems, God sees as solutions'; and what we have to do ... is to wait in peace and refuse to be hustled. 'Fear not, stand still ... and sooner or later you will see the salvation of the Lord' (Exodus 14:13)."

Amy was trying to praise instead of being overwhelmed by disappointment, to erect stepping stones instead of stumbling blocks, and to wait for the Lord to act rather than give way to fear and panic. It is marvelous that she committed so many of her thoughts and meditations to paper so they could be collected up and used to inspire other pilgrims along life's highway. She was not afraid to let people know about her own doubts and shortcomings. Equally, she was always anxious to point out in her writing how her God was the God of the impossible and could deal with every human situation.

Naturally, it gave her a great deal of pleasure when Godfey's elder brother, Dr. Murray, came on a visit to Dohnavur also en route to China. No one could have been more welcome. Amy's first contact with the family had been with the two brothers' grandfather, who in his time was a speaker at Keswick. Their personalities proved different, Murray more lively and Godfrey of a quieter disposition, but both radiated the love of Christ in their lives and drew people to them wherever they went.

Murray's arrival helped in a practical way. There only remained one doctor in Dohnavur, Dr. May Powell, and she was involved with intensive language study, which cut down the time she could spare for surgery. Even though he had come as a visitor, a small operating room was quickly set up and the two doctors immediately embarked on a series of much needed operations. Murray also spent time at Neyyoor to Amy's delight, because she felt she owed them a big debt of gratitude.

On his return, Murray accompanied Amy on visits to many towns and villages in the area. Bishop Frank Houghton quotes a characteristic comment of Amy's on the subject: "We had glorious raids on the kingdom of darkness together," she exulted. The time passed all too quickly and

Murray proved his worth in every activity in which he engaged. Amy watched him go with a heavy heart, seeing clearly how he and his brother could fill the pressing need at Dohnavur. "Let me not covet my neighbor's goods—nor his menservants. Murray and Godfrey are China's menservants. Lord, help and forgive."

She paid the first installment on the land for the boys' compound without having anyone in view to run it.

10

The Place of Heavenly Healing

Amy's heart warmed to Mrs. Webb-Peploe also. In *Gold Cord* she wrote, "Our guests came and went; to that mother we gave an Indian name by which she is known and loved by all our household now—Aruthal, which means Comfort, and we were in need of comfort then."

Another significant comment in her diary as she put down the first amount of money to buy land for the boys' compound, "New land for boys—first advance paid. Help will come. Our God hath not forsaken us." "A foreign land draws us nearer God. He is the only one whom we know here . . . that was how Robert Murray McCheyne felt in the unknown world of Genoa; and in life, I think, we often find ourselves in a foreign land." So often Amy quoted from the lives of other missionary stalwarts in her writings. She obviously

96

derived great comfort in inspirations from their enterprises, just as her Sisterhood of the Common Life drew strength and wisdom from reading the works of the mystics. Amy was humble enough to acknowledge her debt to the great saints and warriors of God who had gone on before.

Strangely enough, on the day she paid the money, September 24, God was beginning to work in the life of Godfrey far away in China. Amy was to know nothing definite of this for nearly three more months, but a cable arrived from Murray asking if his mother and Godfrey could come. Godfrey's health was threatened and he had been ordered a long rest. Dohnavur seemed a natural choice—a peaceful and quiet atmosphere in which to relax but not too far away from China for his return after convalescence if it should be required.

Naturally, Amy was overjoyed to welcome her two dear friends again, but she dared not attach too much significance to it. God stirred her to pray for both Murray and Godfrey for future leadership, but she still had no confirmation. Unknown to her, Godfrey wrote to the CSSM in China resigning from the work there. The Lord had spoken to him on many occasions in that country and always, he found out later, when there was particularly pressing need at Dohnavur. Still he waited to inform Amy until he had an official acknowledgement of his letter.

On the morning of December 15 came a note from Godfrey offering to join the Dohnavur Fellowship. Humbly he wrote, "I don't feel one little bit fit to join you all . . . but, I pray God may make me walk worthy of His high calling." Amy, needless to say, was elated. The children shared her joy and referred to Godfrey as her great birthday present because her celebration fell on the next day, December 16. A truly memorable event—and a partnership that was to last more than twenty-two years. We will never know why God allowed him to go first to China, but Amy herself felt convinced that she was destined for missionary life in Japan, yet her life's main work took place in India.

Amy still went on praying for Murray, as the Lord had told her to do. She and Godfrey shared a natural anxiety over Murray's welfare. A civil war that had been waging in China began to escalate, and the Nationalist armies headed for the Yangtze River. On their route lay Hangchow, the city where Murray was stationed, so he stood in the immediate line of danger. "Again that urge to pray for Murray," reads Amy's diary. The next day the news reached them that Hangchow had fallen, then later they heard that Murray had reached Shanghai in safety together with other colleagues and was waiting there.

Eventually, after it seemed unlikely that it would be safe to return to Hangchow for some time, Murray traveled to Dohnavur for six months' furlough. Amy's diary entry—"My Father, how can I thank Thee enough?"

Even then, it was far from clear that Murray had left China for good. Amy could presume nothing but just be glad that he had been spared through the fighting and had come to join them for the time being. The year wore on and December 15 brought the first anniversary of Godfrey throwing in his lot with them. Amy carried on with her manifold tasks for the children, and her visits with the Starry Cluster to surrounding villages, wondering when God was going to say "Yes." It was not until July 13, 1928, that instead of her own handwriting in the diary was a note pasted in a different script, "May I stay here? Murray."—a triumphant enclosure.

Why did God cause Amy the tension of waiting so long to gain the two men she felt were ideally suited to lead the boys' work at Dohnavur? Again, we can only conjecture. Perhaps she needed to develop a greater degree of patience and trust. "Man's extremity is God's opportunity," the saying goes. Sometimes it is only when human beings get to the end of their own resources that God steps in. Amy at that moment was well content. A more self-important person might have been anxious to keep her hands alone on the reins of government and organization, but Amy was only too happy to delegate responsibilities to those devoted members of staff the Lord had obviously chosen for her.

With the future of the boys' work assured, Amy's thoughts turned once more to the urgent need for a hospital. As early as January 1921, Amy stood with a few friends in the sunset, looking over the plain. "We . . . thought of the people in the scattered villages and towns, and of their need of skilled and loving succor . . . we asked for a place of healing for the people, and for a doctor to lead our boys and girls out into this loving service." At that time the only hospitals were two days' journey distant, to be reached either through intense heat or heavy monsoon rain.

Of course, the advent of motor vehicles eventually shortened the journey, but very sick people and emergency cases needed instant attention. In so many parts of the world the Christian gospel went hand in hand with devoted medical care. People were attracted to Christ because of the loving attitude of doctors and nurses. Amy often wondered why that part of Southern India was devoid of a medical mission when there were so many cases of extreme need waiting for attention.

After the sunset episode, Amy made a written account of the incident in her logbook. At least, the wish had been recorded in words and become a subject for united prayer. The leaders with special responsibility at Dohnavur not only prayed for a building but also for a man to oversee the whole enterprise. Amy herself debated whether she should ask for the gift of healing, and this was actually granted to her in a measure for a short while. Several of the workers and children received relief from pain and suffering through Amy's hands being laid on them.

Obviously, when the healings ceased after just over a year, the Lord was indicating that He had other methods in mind. Far from feeling disappointed, Amy accepted the change as God's will for that time and that situation. She saw the danger of being regarded just as a neighborhood miracle-worker. It might attract the wrong sort of person and certainly might detract from the main purpose of the work at Dohnavur. Amy was always one to shun the limelight. Like John the Baptist she felt it more fitting that "He should increase and I should decrease" (John 3:30). No doubt she would have agreed with the lines of the hymn that says, "To God be the glory, great things He has done." This proved a problem when she was writing. Amy longed to share her vision with interested friends and supporters but she shrank from promoting herself and drawing attention to any of her achievements.

Having made the decision to go forward with plans for a hospital, all was not yet smooth sailing. The fellowship had welcomed the arrival of Dr. May Powell but deplored the fact that two others doctors had found it necessary to return home. The first large check for the hospital arrived in August 1927. One hundred pounds may seem paltry today, but at that time it represented a considerable sum and strengthened Amy's resolve to purchase the land a few months later.

"Place of Heavenly Healing" was the name designated for the as yet nonexistent hospital. Yet no one doubted that it would be built one day, although the possible high cost of the project proved a little intimidating at first. People began to question the sum needed but Amy was adamant, "It must be . . . perfect for its purpose of glorifying the God of love, so that men and women will be drawn to Him. He is also the God of beauty, and it follows that ugliness jars." Beauty was always important to Amy. She saw to it that the nurseries were functional but attractive, that the children wore bright-colored clothing whenever they could afford it, and that as many lovely flowers as possible grew in the gardens. The children were taught to appreciate natural beauty when they visited the Forest House, Three Pavilions, or Joppa, each offering a different view of nature's loveliness.

Before the hospital was built, the medical staff had to make do with an Indian house with four mat huts outside called Suha Vasal—the Door of Health. Although far from adequate, its walls nevertheless witnessed many miracles of healing brought about by the devotion and single-mindedness of the doctors and nurses.

Much discussion took place about the plans for the new building. "Do you think we could manage without a maternity ward at first?" asked Dr. May Powell, not that she didn't want one badly, but because she knew corners would have to be cut. Her nursing colleagues thought it would be absolutely essential to include one, so they left the matter for the Lord's overruling guidance. If He wanted one, He would cause the money to be sent.

Amy vividly recounted the story of the first check for £1,000. It arrived on a family feast day when the children sat down on the floor with delicacies piled on a green leaf plate in front of each guest and garlands of bright flowers festooned the walls above their heads. In *Gold Cord* Amy wrote,

". . . a child ran up with a yellow envelope in her hand . . . I opened it quickly and read, 'One thousand pounds for maternity ward' . . . I stood like Rhoda, and opened not the gate for gladness."

A great deal of the money came in tiny amounts, often contributed by the children themselves. With remarkable self-sacrifice for such young boys and girls, they earned small amounts by undertaking various tasks and, although they could quite easily have spent it on themselves because very little money ever passed through their fingers, they gladly gave Amy their "widow's mite" to swell the funds for the hospital, just like the lady in the story Jesus told in Luke 21.

Apart from the pressing need for the extra space and equipment for seriously ill patients, Amy could see a further use for a hospital—a by-product perhaps from the main purpose, but it still might prove most rewarding. It was never easy to obtain training and jobs for the boys and girls rescued when young and then brought up at Dohnavur. Naturally, Amy wished them to remain in a sympathetic, Christian atmosphere when they became adults, but suitable openings were few and far between. However, if they could be trained as hospital staff—from porters, cooks, and assistant workers to nurses, doctors and even perhaps surgeons, it would be a worthwhile objective. They would create a skilled, reliable source of recruits.

Amy too had further aims for the new hospital. "Our chief evangelistic field . . . is surely the Parama Suha Salai, with all its contacts." It had become evident over the years that even the limited amount of medical treatment they had been able to carry out had brought immeasurable results in evangelistic outreach. People who normally would not have darkened their doors flocked in great numbers when faced with health problems that their own priests and quack miracle workers could not touch. Their hearts were reached first by the loving, caring attitude of the medical staff rather than with the spoken gospel message. Gradually the patients realized that these Christians lived out practically what they believed, and in gratitude for the kindness they had received, they listened more attentively to the story of Jesus Christ, the Great Healer himself.

Although unanimously delighted that the actual building of the hospital had started, the Dohnavur staff did not see the completion for several years. They carried on gallantly in the crowded Suha Vasal—the Door of Health—under difficult conditions. The work put everyone under considerable physical pressure because of the lack of suitable space. Amy was always sensitive to the needs of her staff and anxious to lighten their load. Early on in the year of 1931 she felt strongly that Murray needed a short spell of leave to refresh him and prepare him for all the extra duties that would arise once the hospital was ready for occupation. Consulting Dr. May Powell, Amy found that May shared her opinion, so she passed on her conviction to Murray that he should take a time for rest and relaxation. In view of the two women's joint agreement on the subject, he felt happy to go and made arrangements to leave in June. He might not have acquiesced so willingly had he received any advance premonition of the trouble that would befall the founder of the work after his departure.

11

A New Battle

*I*n battle you need soldiers who fear nothing"
was a favorite quotation of Amy's from *The
Spiritual Letters of Fire Didon.*
A stanza from one of her poems runs like this:

Make us Thy warriors
*On whom Thou canst depend to stand the
brunt*
Of any perilous charge on any front;
Give to us skill to handle sword and spear,
*From the rising of the morning till the stars
appear.*

Amy often used military terminology when she
wrote or spoke about her life's work. She was bat-
tling not only against evil men and women who
sought the moral destruction of innocent children
but against "the wicked spiritual forces in the
heavenly world, the rulers, authorities and cosmic
powers of this dark age" (Eph. 6:12, Good News

106

Bible). It is significant that the next verse reads, "So put on God's armor now!" Amy knew well the comfort and protection of that heavenly armor, the sword of the Spirit and the helmet of salvation.

When Bishop Frank Houghton wrote Amy's biography, he divided it into three sections. The middle one, which started with the story of the first Temple child acquired, "The Warfare of the Service," related Amy's long and valiant fight on behalf of her precious children. The final section of the book, from 1931 onward, he called "The Keeping of the Charge." What happened in that year to switch Amy from a physically active role into a more passive one?

Just before the incident—the accident—that led up to it is described, it would be well worthwhile to quote two more historical anecdotes that Amy mentioned in her book of readings *Thou Givest . . . They Gather*. When the Crusaders had landed on enemy territory with the sea at their backs, their leader knew they would be tempted to re-embark in their boats drawn up along the shore if the going proved difficult. So he had the boats burned to prevent any means of retreat, leaving no possibility of escape.

She also told how Philip of Macedon, the father of Alexander the Great, when his soldiers were storming a walled city, had the storming ladders removed from behind them when they reached the top of the wall. They had to conquer or die. Amy asked this question of her own work: "Have we any boats unburned? any ladder not flung down?

Boats and ladders—what are they? They are ways of retreat from difficult things, from fights with the great enemy of souls.''

Amy had always been one to confront difficulties and meet them head on—all the more remarkable because of her physical weakness at the start of her missionary service. She had experienced years of sheer, concentrated, hard work and also persecution from the Temple officials who resented her rescuing children at risk from their immoral practices. She had known the heartache of losing dear children from childhood diseases and trusted, valued, older helpers like Ponnammal. There had never existed a surplus of money. God had always been faithful, but at times their food stocks had run perilously low. Since her arrival in India, she had never traveled back to England on furlough. Sometimes she had wondered if she would ever be sent sufficient workers of the right caliber to carry out her plans.

Although God had never let her down, the years from 1901 to 1931 had taken their toll on her. She had become very weary but not dispirited; there was always a message of comfort to be found for her in God's Word. "Have you ever felt, I have had enough of fighting; I want a lull; I want peace from turmoil? If so, read this story about Eleazar, one of David's mighty men, who, when he was left alone, (for the men of Israel were gone away) he arose and fought until his hand was weary, and . . . clave unto the sword (he was too tired to do anything but just hold on). Many of us do not have to fight alone even as to outward help; we have comrades who never desert us in a hard place."

At times she felt too weary to carry out her usual routine, but she always tried to hide the fact from others. With an eye to the future, she held a discussion with as many members of her staff as possible, although Murray was away and Godfrey ill, and was very relieved to discover that they were all of one mind that the two brothers would eventually become the leaders on the men's side and May Powell on the women's side.

Further meetings were held and amazingly it was decided to pray for more helpers—doctors, a pharmacist, and a teacher. Everyone felt the urgency to take the gospel to those who had never heard it, even though their leader was worn out and their financial resources low. "Funds short, the very time to look for an advance" was the entry in the logbook. Amy had never been one to resist a challenge, and she had inspired her team to adopt a similar attitude. Shortage of funds was no signal for retreat. On August 6 of that year a monthly Day of Prayer was held and all present in Amy's small room showed their willingness to make fresh efforts to reach the many thousands of Muslims and Hindus who lived in that part of India.

Within a couple of months two towns had been chosen as immediate targets, and Amy described the problems of gaining a foothold in both towns in some considerable detail in *Gold Cord*. Weaker, more fearful mortals would have withdrawn in the early weeks; there was very little to encourage them. In Eruvadi (or Song of the Plough) stones were thrown right inside the rooms that the workers at Dohnavur had occupied. The men were definitely hostile to the whole project. As usual, God had the last word in spite of strong opposition. The mother of a man who had stirred up the locals at a meeting to drive the Christians out had a painful carbuncle treated by the sisters, and their loving attitude quite won him over.

In Kalakadu (or Joyous City) the only housing that could be obtained had been thought to be haunted by an evil spirit for some time. Although on the surface a most undesirable dwelling, the workers from Dohnavur rejoiced to gain a foothold in the town. Amy never intended to remain a remote figurehead making decisions but holding back from becoming really involved. Time and again she visited the house to check on the improvements being made for her staff's welfare and to see the progress for herself.

On September 24, Amy prayed early in the morning, "Do with me as Thou wilt. Do anything, Lord, that will fit me to serve Thee and help my beloveds." It must have required a great deal of courage to give expression to such a petition. How would God answer this prayer? She could not have guessed the answer.

And shall I pray Thee change Thy will my
*   Father,*
Until it be according to mine?
But no, Lord, no, that never shall be, rather

*I pray Thee blend my human will with
    Thine.*

Within a few short hours Amy was to learn His surprising, amazing will for the rest of her life. Late in the afternoon she made another car journey to Kalakadu to satisfy herself about the progress of the work. A delay occurred in getting hold of the key for the house. As it was growing later, the daylight began to disappear. Amy failed to see a pit some workmen had dug in an area where none was planned, and taken unaware in the dim light she slipped.

Everyone in the Family was distressed and concerned for Amy. It was impossible to visualize life without Amy organizing and remaining at the helm. Although her injuries were far from slight, most members were optimistic that she would once more shoulder the majority of her normal duties as soon as the healing process had taken place. Surely God must have some purpose in allowing it, but it wouldn't last forever. Good would surely come out of the seeming tragedy . . . or would it? Time alone would tell.

As soon as the news got around, the people from the town crowded outside the house, predicting that the accident had been caused by the evil spirit who had been haunting the house for so long. The Muslims in Eruvadi put forward a theory that the curse of Allah had fallen upon Amy for opposing the forces of Islam. Amy had to wait there until help came from Dohnavur to rush her the forty-six miles to Neyyoor. There her old friend and ally Dr. Howard Somervell set her leg in plaster. She was finally allowed to return home on November 3. It probably seemed a long ten days to Amy, but her leg had been broken and her ankle dislocated. In addition, she was now sixty-four years old and bones take longer to heal at that stage of life than in a younger person. "Home. Goodness and Mercy" was her short and succinct phrase in her logbook that evening.

Unfortunately, the pain lingered on rather than fading out, which meant that Amy suffered many sleepless nights. Naturally, a great deal of time was spent in prayer on her behalf. Special times—or days—were set aside just for that purpose, and one day in January the Family arranged a nonstop chain of prayer from 6:00 A.M. to 9:00 P.M. Occasionally people were allowed into her room for a brief glimpse of her, and she continued to prepare messages, but they were usually delivered on her behalf by someone else who had been delegated. She even began to be taken out by car from time to time, but basically her period of active physical service was over. Rather like Florence Nightingale who spent most of the years after her involvement in the Crimea campaign as a semi-invalid in bed, Amy rarely left her room for nearly twenty years.

As time passed, other symptoms began to appear. Quite likely she had jarred her spine in the fall because acute neuritis made one arm virtually useless, and arthritis settled in her back. Occasionally she would fall victim to chronic infections. She might have come through this period with much less trouble and fewer side effects had she not already been worn out—not only physically but emotionally—after years of strain, tension, and at times, even physical danger at the hands of violent antagonists.

Amy had been a trailblazer, a pioneer among women, pitting her strength against Satanic forces in Southern India. Never robust in health from her early missionary days, she pushed herself to the limit month after month, year after year. It is helpful to remember how the emancipation of women has progressed since the turn of the century. Amy had no precedent to follow when she took on her arduous task, and she drew a great deal of criticism from people who preferred their women to be decorative, of little practical ability, and with a shallow, unquestioning mind.

People might be forgiven for imagining that Amy lived the sequestered, cushioned existence of an invalid from 1931 onward. Sometimes, it is true, her staff tried to shield her from some of the crises and upheavals that befell Dohnavur over the years. Basically, she still felt committed both to the work so close to her heart and the wider aspect of the spread of the Christian gospel throughout the world and continued to work to that end. On bad days pain took over and she had to retire from battle for a while. Then she would rally again and surprise everyone.

It may be trite to quote the old adage, "The pen is mightier than the sword," but the pen certainly proved a powerful weapon in Amy's hands. It is never wise to speculate why God allowed a certain event to happen, because mere onlookers do not possess the inside knowledge to weigh up the situation, but undoubtedly the Christian community worldwide would have been infinitely the poorer without the hundreds of letters and thirteen entire books she wrote after 1931.

Her letters were sent out to a wide range of people. Always when her own staff were away on furlough, like Murray and Godfrey, she kept communicating with them so they would still feel in touch with the "home base" of Dohnavur. To her it seemed important that they should not return to an unknown situation where various developments had taken place without their knowledge. Being kept informed would help them feel perfectly in tune with the rest of the staff.

But they didn't have to wait until they had traveled many hundreds of miles before a letter from Amy reached them. Constantly she had delivered to many of her helpers short notes of appreciation for services rendered or helpful advice over a tricky problem. Letters were written in both Tamil and English but not always by Amy's own hand. Sometimes when she felt too tired to make the effort herself, one of her companions would pen the words at her dictation, but it still retained its personal character.

At other times, small Indian boys and girls would rejoice to receive a written message on their birthdays and Coming Days and would treasure the tiny scrap of paper long afterward until it had become worn and creased with the words almost obliterated. Amy achieved a great deal of success with her children because she treated them as individuals. No one was made to feel institutionalized. Each was conscious of a unique, personal link with his beloved Amma.

Besides the new books Amy wrote after being confined to bed, she was responsible for preparing several older works for new editions. Her poetry remained a conscious source of joy for her. Inspiration came in the days of pain and suffering just as it had done in her former busy, active life. Some verses were set to music and sung at Family prayers. It seemed as though God had a special purpose in removing Amy from normal daily duties, because her concentrated period of writing proved such a blessing to so many readers throughout the world.

12

The Final Curtain

During this period Amy received a cable of encouragement from Australia with the simple message, "And the light shined in the cell." It referred originally, of course, to the episode when an angel appeared to Peter in prison to set him free, but Amy took this text as it was intended and it brought great comfort to her, although she was largely confined to her own single room. She was comforted by the message so much that she wrote a short song on the theme with Mabel Wade supplying the music—a truly poignant set of verses under the circumstances.

> And a light shined in the cell
> And there was not any wall,
> And there was no dark at all,
> Only Thou, Immanuel.

In a very real way Amy was conscious of God's presence with her throughout that long confinement in her sickroom. No doubt she would rather have been engaged in her former hectic schedule, but her bodily strength had been failing, and the enforced rest gave her a chance to conserve her energies and concentrate them on the tasks she could still perform.

If visits had to be rationed to spare her, Amy usually found a moment to converse with anyone who was in doubt, difficulty, or danger of any kind. She still liked to be accessible to those in need of guidance or assistance.

Godfrey took over the main writing of the Dohnavur letter giving news of the fellowship to friends and supporters. Sometimes it contained short messages from her and usually, although Amy herself was unwilling to gain personal publicity, a brief bulletin on the state of her health. Readers avidly devoured all the news but missed Amy's significant contributions to the publication. In 1933 came the answer to their pleas: *Dust of Gold*, written by Amy herself, with details of life at Dohnavur and what God was doing for them in His own inimitable way. Both newsletters were welcomed and appreciated by supporters for a couple of years until it was finally decided to concentrate solely on *Dust of Gold* to spare Godfrey the extra effort in his already busy schedule. Amazingly, Amy produced this largely single-handed until 1948.

The times when she did leave her room were red-letter days on Amy's calendar. It might be a visit to the House of Prayer, to a wedding, or to the

Place of Heavenly Healing. Sometimes she was even carried as far as the Forest to make a welcome change for her, but the occasions did not happen very often. Yet they were all the more precious because of that. Now she herself was in need of constant medical attention; how glad she must have been that she had been instrumental in constructing the Dohnavur hospital, giving to many sick and needy people in the area, who otherwise would have been deprived of medical care, a chance of healing.

Naturally the layout and decor of Amy's room became important to her as it represented the limits of her small world. The final result embodied utility, orderliness, and yet beauty. Eye appeal had always been important to her, and although denied luxuries as a missionary servant of the Lord, a touch of color within the room and the view outside brought her great aesthetic satisfaction.

The tone was set by a wooden plaque outside saying simply "The Room of Peace."

And this was true of the atmosphere within. "All through these months her room has been a place of peace, of joy and of song." Blue curtains were draped near the door—Amy was still faithful to her favorite color from early times—and bookcases full of all sorts of volumes lined the walls in that area, freely available for the rest of the household to borrow. "They are my great luxury, my mental change of air." Although confined in one room, and often attacked by pain, Amy still possessed an interest in and a vision for the whole world outside. She welcomed the challenge of new ideas that literature brought to her. Another favorite feature, although just outside the window, was a small aviary with colorful birds flitting from branch to branch, bringing both pleasure to her and many small visitors. Favorite pictures decorated her walls, delighting her eyes and stimulating her thoughts and imagination.

This was the nerve center of Dohnavur. Naturally the task of active, physical leadership was carried out by the two Webb-Peploe brothers, Dr. May Powell, and Arulai, and Amy was more than content that it should be so. Yet all returned to that one room upon occasions for inspiration, benediction, and consultation with the founder of the work.

Amy did not possess a monopoly in bad health. From time to time both Godfrey and Murray gave cause for concern. In 1933 Murray had to travel to Australia for a period of convalescence. Just prior to his leaving, Amy had attended his wedding to Oda van Boelzelaer, the first Dutch member of the fellowship. It was an added bonus when they returned two years later bringing with them their twin boys.

The balance sheet at Dohnavur over the next few years would have shown both profit and loss. Painful misunderstandings arose in England and America over false rumors about the fellowship's alleged involvement with the so-called Oxford Group. This took a good deal of refuting and was totally without foundation. Amy contested this with all her might, stating clearly the simple basis of Christian biblical truth on which Dohnavur had been founded. On the positive side, various baptisms brought them joy, including that of a Muslim couple. A mission carried out by R. T. Archibald and Quintin Carr proved very fruitful, no doubt because the Word was sown on good ground, carefully prepared beforehand by Amy and many members of her staff.

However much others tried to spare her extra pressure, Amy never became a remote figurehead out of touch with the problems of daily life. While unable to be supportive by her physical presence, she prayed over forays by her staff into difficult territory to rescue children from grave moral danger and was all agog to hear the outcome when her staff members returned. She herself even tried to spare others harassment by interviewing difficult people in the privacy of her own room. No one, however, could be shielded from failures and departures, and there were times when everyone, including Amy, felt under strain. On the whole, though, she was loyally supported by her staff. They formed a united team. A note to some helpers away in the Forest read, ". . . O how I love you all . . . I think of you separately, and dwell upon each one in thought and love and thanksgiving."

Of course, as Amy grew older, she mourned for many of her friends of long standing as first one and then the other passed away. Irene Streeter was killed in a plane crash in 1937. After another ten years Mary Hatch, whom she had first met in the early Manchester days, died and was greatly missed. Then, too, the outbreak of the Second World War in 1939 brought great cause for anxiety. On a personal level, friends and loved ones were put in positions of grave danger. At first Dohnavur remained far removed from most theaters of war, but later on as the conflict spread, it seemed quite likely that the Japanese might launch an invasion. Inflation because of wartime scarcity of supplies badly affected their funds. Amy always possessed a large heart for anyone in distress. As in the previous conflict, Amy agonized over the sufferings of the occupied countries. She could never remain unmoved and aloof when fellow human beings were in great danger.

Often she wished to be able to "mother" her family again. Others might possess the professional qualifications—and she greatly admired and gave God thanks for them—but she longed to make her own inimitable contribution to the life of the family.

"The greatest difficulty is to readjust, to see others daily worn down by the Warfare of the Service, and to be oneself sheltered from all the hardest things." Her logbook bore witness to her touches of humor, even in great pain, and to her complete honesty.

Compensations occurred from time to time. Essential renovations to the old bungalow demanded that she had to move out for a while. On her return she found to her delight that a terrace leading from her room to the garden had been constructed, which made it easier for her to meet with a larger number of people. Then another serious setback took place. On June 23, 1948, Amy slipped in her room, damaging her right hip and breaking her right forearm. Friends were anxious that this latest accident would be too much for her frail body.

Always she had been conscious of the prayer support of the whole fellowship. After eight years as an invalid she acknowledged, "For eight years many of you have daily prayed for me, not the ordinary costless prayer—'God bless her'— but something far more vital." These prayers went on as long as she lived, as did her prayers for all the Dohnavur folk. Her prayers, too, like those of her colleagues, were never vague or general but wholeheartedly specific, dealing with particular problems or situations. For instance, she wrote to Murray in 1943, "This day in 1929 . . . I kept the whole Family for two hours in the House of Prayer while you did your first big spectacular operation."

Her literary output was staggering: thirty-five books from 1895 to 1950. Although they sold well and proved popular with the Christian public, that was never Amy's intention or priority. "The truth, whatever people think," was her advice to a young missionary biographer. She was motivated by honesty in her own writing, not seeking to gloss over unpalatable facts. This policy paid off in the end, in spite of advice to the contrary, and many people were stimulated to offer themselves for missionary service, spurred on by the facts revealed in Amy's books. Altogether her books were published in fifteen languages and made for her many friends of varying nationalities. Amy derived much pleasure from the fact that twelve of her books were put into braille in England and eight in the United States. Amy's poems still continued to be greatly appreciated and quite often were put to music for the Family to sing at prayer times. Not all reached the same literary level, but the spiritual thoughts contained in them brought inspiration to many.

As the years advanced, personal sorrows had their effect on Amy. She had felt sure for some time that Arulai was showing such qualities of leadership that she might well become the new leader of the Women's work. "She is perhaps the most precious thing I have on earth," Amy wrote to the doctor in charge of Arulai's case, and yet in May 1939 God called Arulai home to be with himself. Then in February 1947, urgent family reasons caused Murray to return to England, his wife and the twin boys having traveled ahead of him. No one, least of all Murray, would have chosen this step, but it seemed inevitable at the time.

Concealing her own grief, which could not have been easy for a woman of eighty, Amy sought to rally and strengthen those that remained. She knew well that the heaviest burden would fall on Godfrey who, though more than willing, was suffering from a physical disability, resulting in a thrombosis of his right leg. In February 1950, he died suddenly. Amy confessed that her first thoughts had been, "Why am I left—I who am useless to you all—and he, who could do so much for you, taken?" Then she realized that even to think such a thing was sinful. "Faith never wonders why. Faith trusts . . ."

Nevertheless, it was hard for her to accept that three of the possible future leaders of the work had been removed from Dohnavur. "I am left broken but content, safe in the Hand of the mighty and loving One to whom this Fellowship belongs."

Many who witnessed her second fall would have imagined that it would have hastened her end, but she lasted, in great frailty, for nearly another three years. On her better days she still wrote a little, but the effort demanded a great deal from her ebbing strength. Amy dreaded lingering on so long that she would become nothing but a burden to her staff, diverting their energies from more essential tasks. Various friends sent her reassuring texts and verses from hymns to see her through what was surely becoming "the valley of the shadow of death."

"To depart and be with Christ which is far better" (Phil. 1:23) was her sincere longing. But first she had to celebrate her eightieth birthday and then Christmas following soon afterward. Perhaps celebrate is too strong and positive a word, yet Amy lived through both festal days with a quiet sense of thankfulness.

Quietly she sank into a coma by the middle of the first month of the new year. The Family crept in and out, tiptoeing by her bedside for a last glance. Yet there came no final, meaningful message from her lips as some had hoped. Peacefully, she slipped away imperceptibly as she had always wanted—"no rending goodbye, no distress to anyone"—in the early morning hours of January 18, 1951.

For a while she lay in her room and then in the Dohnavur church with a bodyguard of "her men and boys." At the service over one thousand text cards were handed out to the congregation, explaining God's plan of salvation. A more intimate Family service was held in the House of Prayer and then Amy's internment followed.

No elaborately carved headstones distinguish the graves there. Amy's can be recognized by a beautiful stone birdbath put up at the side. She, who gained so much pleasure from watching the birds from the sanctuary of her own room, would have been pleased at that gesture, but how much more pleasure she would have gained in the knowledge that the work would still continue in Southern India. Over the years it has changed slightly in character as different dangers have loomed, but the same motivation and the same dedication, still marks all the helpers in the Dohnavur complex.

From Millisle to Madras came a weak young woman to carry out the task she believed God had assigned to her. After fifty-six years there she departed this life as a frail old lady, but she left behind her a strong and lasting memorial in the hearts of all those whom she rescued from danger and introduced to the "unsearchable riches of Christ."